THE ART & CRAFT OF
Making Jewelry

THE ART & CRAFT OF
Making Jewelry

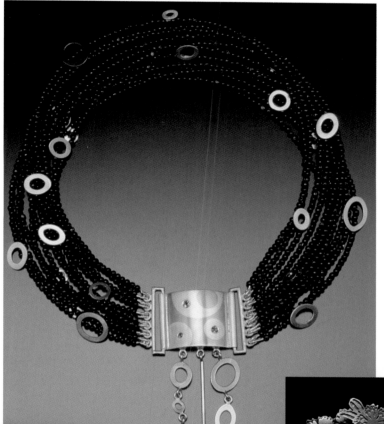

A Complete
Guide to
Essential
Techniques

Joanna Gollberg

LARK BOOKS
A Division of Sterling Publishing Co., Inc.
New York

Editor: Marthe Le Van
Art Director: Kathleen Holmes
Cover Designer: Barbara Zaretsky
Associate Editor: Nathalie Mornu
Associate Art Director: Shannon Yokeley
Editorial Assistance: Delores Gosnell
Editorial Intern: Sue Stigleman
Art Intern: Emily Kepley
Photography: keithwright.com
IIIustrations: Orrin Lundgren
Proofreader: Karen Levy

Library of Congress Cataloging-in-Publication Data

Gollberg, Joanna.
  The art & craft of making jewelry : a complete guide to essential techniques / Joanna Gollberg.
    p. cm.
  Includes index.
  ISBN 1-57990-570-6 (hardcover)
  1. Jewelry making. I. Title. II. Title: Art and craft of making jewelry.
TT212.G64 2006
739.27--dc22
                        2005034040

10 9 8 7 6 5 4 3 2

Published by Lark Books, A Division of Sterling Publishing Co., Inc., 387 Park Avenue South, New York, NY 10016

Text © 2006, Joanna Gollberg
Photography © 2006, Lark Books, unless otherwise noted
Illustrations © 2006, Lark Books

Distributed in Canada by Sterling Publishing, c/o Canadian Manda Group, 165 Dufferin Street
Toronto, Ontario, Canada M6K 3H6

Distributed in the United Kingdom by GMC Distribution Services, Castle Place, 166 High Street, Lewes,
East Sussex, England BN7 1XU

Distributed in Australia by Capricorn Link (Australia) Pty Ltd., P.O. Box 704, Windsor, NSW 2756 Australia

If you have questions or comments about this book, please contact:
Lark Books, 67 Broadway, Asheville, NC 28801, (828) 253-0467

Manufactured in China

ISBN 13: 978-1-57990-570-5
ISBN 10: 1-57990-570-6

For information about custom editions, special sales, and premium and corporate purchases, please contact
Sterling Special Sales Department at 800-805-5489 or specialsales@sterlingpub.com.

Contents

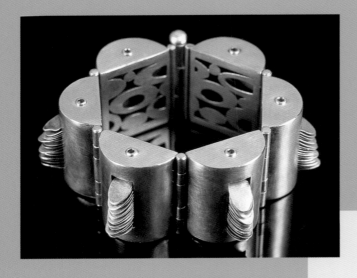

Introduction

The Art and Craft of Making Jewelry is an easy-to-follow
resource anyone can use to learn an extensive range of
jewelry techniques, from basic sawing, piercing, and
riveting to advanced hollow forms, stone setting, and
surface embellishment. This book is unique because it
thoroughly and concisely explains essential metalworking skills in a practical step-by-step process so you can
achieve real, tangible results. Each technique is
enhanced with color photographs that provide clear and
effective instruction.

Every chapter is supplemented with projects, so you can
produce wearable jewelry using the techniques you've
learned. You can copy the designs exactly or simply use
them as a springboard for other projects. Jewelry is
personal—for the wearer as a means of expressing per-
sonality, and for the maker as a means of expressing
him- or herself—so I encourage you to mix techniques
and invent original pieces. Let the instructions be a creative catalyst. To challenge and inspire you, images of
contemporary jewelry are included throughout the book.
These show how the topics being discussed are used by
today's leading jewelers.

With practice, anyone can learn the techniques
described in this book, but no one will master them
right away. If your skills feel shaky or your projects
don't look the way you want them to on your first
attempt, stay positive. Remember that everything
undertaken in life improves with practice. One of the
pleasures of making something beautiful and well

crafted is knowing the hard work that has gone into it. If you want to make high-quality jewelry, you can. The key is to remain optimistic and keep working.

An important element in the creative process is to execute each job as best you can. A good jewelry design that is not well executed does not live up to its potential, so take care to keep your standards up and produce jewelry that is of the highest quality. Clasps should always work easily and securely. Solder seams should always be tight. All firescale should be removed from each piece. All finishing should be beautiful and intentional. You want to be proud of what you create, and you want others to be proud to wear your work.

This last piece of advice is simple but significant—have fun! It is obvious to others when your jewelry does not include a sense of joy. If the work you are doing is not fun and meaningful to you, figure out a different way to do it, or move on to something else. Some techniques in this book may be very appealing to you while others may be less so. Concentrate on the ones that feel good and delve into them with passion. Making jewelry can be such a wonderful way to spend time, and I hope this book will help you do so in a challenging and delightful way.

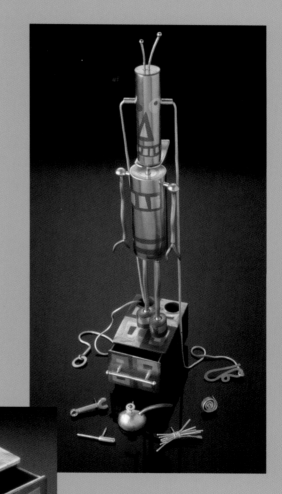

Metals & Their Properties

There are many types of metals readily available for jewelry making. This survey concentrates on those most often used in the jewelry industry and by craftspeople, but it also touches on some metals that can be used in nontraditional jewelry.

There are two main groups of metal: ferrous metals contain iron, while nonferrous metals do not contain iron. Within the nonferrous metal category is a subgroup called noble metals. In their raw state, these metals are unchanged by elements in the air. Examples of noble metals include silver, gold, and platinum, considered by our society to be precious metals. Base metals and alloys are other subgroups of nonferrous metals.

Precious metals: 18-karat gold, sterling silver

Precious Metals

Most jewelry is created from an alloy form of these metals. Refer to figure 5 on page 14 for precise melting points and specific gravities.

Gold

Of all metals, gold is the most malleable. This means that it can be worked for the longest amount of time without cracking. When flattened to 0.000005 inch (0.13 micrometers), gold becomes a thin foil, almost transparent to light. Gold is also the most ductile of all metals, meaning that 1 ounce (28.4 g) of pure gold can be drawn into a wire several miles (km) long.

Silver

Silver is second to gold in its malleability and ductility. It also has the ability to be highly polished and reflective, and it is resistant to corrosion. Although silver is the best conductor of electricity, copper is more frequently used for this purpose in industrial applications due to its relative cost.

Platinum

Platinum is malleable and ductile and resists corrosion. It has a high specific gravity and an attractive dark gray color, which is appealing to many wearers. The durability of platinum makes it very popular in the jewelry industry, especially for use with precious stones.

Palladium, ruthenium, rhodium, osmium, and iridium are by-products of platinum ore. Palladium and ruthenium are often used in platinum alloys. The addition of these metals can make platinum lighter, which is useful for making large jewelry items, and can increase platinum's hardness and strength.

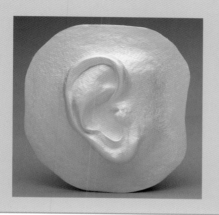

Base Metals

In addition to gold, silver, and platinum, base metals are the most commonly used metals in jewelry making. A beginner will find them inexpensive and easy to work with while learning new skills and techniques. These metals provide many different color choices that can add interesting effects. Soldering base metals is basically the same as soldering precious metals; although they have different melting points, (see figure 5, page 14) they can be used in combination with ease.

Base metals, clockwise from top: aluminum, copper, nickel silver, brass

Brass

Brass, an alloy of copper and zinc, is quite malleable and is resistant to corrosion. Some brass alloys, such as NuGold, have higher amounts of copper (approximately 88 percent copper and 12 percent zinc) and are richer in color.

Copper

Copper was the first metal known to man. It retains a high polish, but it is quite susceptible to oxidation from the natural atmosphere. Copper conducts electricity very well and it has good working properties, meaning it is malleable and can be worked both hot and cold.

Bronze

Bronze, an alloy of copper and tin, is slightly more orange-red in color than brass. It is easily melted and cast, and it is less susceptible to corrosion than its parent metal, copper.

Nickel Silver

Nickel silver is a very inexpensive alloy of copper (60 percent), nickel (20 percent), and zinc (20 percent). It has a rich gray color similar to that of white gold. This alloy is used in jewelry making because it is relatively malleable and has good working properties. Since many people are allergic to nickel silver, however, it is not a good idea to use it for earring findings or for jewelry that will have a lot of contact with the skin, such as rings. Nickel silver can also be challenging to solder because it oxidizes quickly, and this oxidation can be difficult to remove.

Aluminum

Aluminum, a lightweight metal that is very white in color, is quite malleable, ductile, and resistant to corrosion. It can also be *anodized*. In this process, a resistant oxide film is created on the surface of aluminum by electricity. This film can then be dyed in an array of appealing colors. Although aluminum can be joined with heat through welding and soldering, it is best fabricated with cold connections.

Titanium

Titanium, a lightweight metal with a gray-brown color, is a ductile and tough metal that is resistant to corrosion. Titanium cannot be soldered, but it can be cold joined.

Niobium

Niobium is a soft, ductile metal that polishes well and, like aluminum, it can be anodized. This metal cannot be soldered but can be cold connected.

Lead

Due to its toxicity and its ability to ruin other metals, lead is no longer used in jewelry making, and I recommend that all lead be kept out of your studio. The only time lead should be used in jewelry making is in the alloy called *niello*, a mixture of sterling silver, lead, and sulfur. This alloy produces a soft, dark gray metal used as a surface design inlay.

Pewter

Light gray in color and quite attractive when polished, pewter is a great choice for making large metal pieces, such as boxes or containers, but should be used separately from the more precious metals due to contamination issues. Pewter can be soldered with a very low-temperature, lead-free solder and a soldering iron instead of a torch.

Alloys

There are many reasons for creating and using metal alloys. Strength and durability top the list, but making alloys to change the color of metal is also popular.

Sterling Silver

Sterling silver is 92.5 percent silver and 7.5 percent copper. The copper is added to the silver in its pure form (99.9 percent silver) to increase strength. This fact, combined with its beauty, is what makes sterling silver popular for hollowware and cutlery as well as jewelry.

White Gold

White gold is lighter than platinum but darker than sterling silver in appearance. This alloy is made by adding nickel or palladium to pure gold. Nickel white gold is harder to work with than palladium white gold because nickel is a harder metal. Furthermore, nickel white gold often produces problems with firescale, making cleaning much more difficult. Palladium white gold is a pleasure to work with because it is easier to form and leaves no firescale.

Yellow Gold

Yellow gold is made by adding silver and copper to pure gold, and the more copper that is added, the redder the metal will become. The working properties of yellow gold vary depending on the percentages of the alloy.

Green Gold

Green gold is made with pure gold and 30 to 40 percent silver, cadmium, and zinc. This alloy is quite malleable and easy to work with.

Gold Filled

The term *gold filled* does not refer to an alloy. It means that a thin layer of gold has been soldered or otherwise mechanically adhered to a layer of base metal, commonly brass or silver, and then drawn or flattened to a specific dimension.

Karats

In the United States, a measurement called a *karat* is used to specify the purity of gold. As shown in figure 1 (page 11), gold alloys are organized into different karats based on their proportions of gold (the classification is based on 24ths). Twenty-four-karat gold represents the metal in its purest form. Although it is has the richest orange-yellow color, 24-karat gold is also the softest gold. Eighteen-

karat gold is harder and more durable than 24-karat gold. It is available in many colors and is easy to work with. Both 14-karat gold and 12-karat gold are duller in color than the higher karats, but they are most commonly used in commercial jewelry in the United States due to their relative cost. European countries do not allow the use of 14-karat or 12-karat gold in jewelry. Their measurement system, based on parts of gold per 1000, is detailed in figure 1, column 3.

Different gold suppliers use slightly different alloys for making various karats and colors. I recommend that you use the same gold supplier to maintain consistency in the color and character of the metal.

Japanese Alloys

Popular in modern art jewelry, the Japanese alloys shakudo and shibuishi are often used in techniques such as mokume gane and marriage of metal. Shakudo contains 95 percent silver and 5 percent gold, and it melts between 1968° and 1980°F (1075.5° and 1082.2°C). Shibuishi is 75 percent copper and 25 percent silver, and it melts at 1775°F (968.3°C). These alloys take a patina well, and they can be turned a rich, deep black. They are both quite malleable and have excellent working properties.

Solders

Solders are alloys of precious metals that have lower melting points than the specific metals they are intended to join. This allows solder to be heated to its flow point without melting the principal metal. More information on solder can be found on pages 26 and 27.

Silver Solder

Silver solder is an alloy of silver, copper, and zinc. It is produced in alloys with different melting temperatures, allowing jewelers to perform consecutive solderings on a single piece without melting the previously soldered joint (see figure 2). Silver solders are most commonly available in easy flow, easy, medium, hard, and IT varieties. Easy-flow silver solder flows at the lowest temperature, and the higher the melting point of the solder, the more silver there is in the alloy. Silver solder is also used for soldering copper, brass, bronze, and nickel.

Gold Solder

Gold solders are produced in all karats (proportions) and in temperatures similar to those of silver solders. Gold solders are generally made from an alloy of gold with an addition of fine silver. Often cadmium is added to the solder to lower its melting point. Due to its expense, gold solder is mostly used only for soldering gold pieces.

FIGURE 1
Percentage of Gold in Karat Alloys

PERCENTAGE OF GOLD	KARAT	PARTS PER 1000
100	24	1000
91.67	22	916
75	18	750
58.33	14	583
50	12	500

FIGURE 2
Silver Solder Melting & Flow Temperatures*

SOLDER TYPE	APPROXIMATE MELTING POINT	APPROXIMATE FLOW POINT
Extra Easy	1145°F (618°C)	1207°F (653°C)
Easy	1240°F (682°C)	1325°F (718°C)
Medium	1275°F (691°C)	1360°F (738°C)
Hard	1365°F (741°C)	1450°F (788°C)
IT	1340°F (726°C)	1490°F (810°C)

*Temperatures vary from manufacturer to manufacturer.
Ask for product specifications with your order.

Ferrous Metals

Using ferrous metals in jewelry can be very interesting, especially when the unique properties of these metals are exploited. The rusting and aging of ferrous metals can produce interesting colors and surface textures. Ferrous metals may be cold joined or welded.

Ferrous metal sheet, rod, and wire

Iron

Iron is a tough metal that is very brittle in its pure form and prone to corrosion. The rust resulting from oxidation can be used as an interesting surface coloring for jewelry, but it should be sealed to prevent the rust from getting onto clothing. Although iron can be cast, it cannot be bent, soldered, sawn, filed, or drilled, so it is best used as a found object element in jewelry.

Steel

Steel, an alloy of iron and carbon, is capable of being tempered (heat treated) to many different degrees of hardness.

Stainless Steel

Stainless steel is an alloy of steel, chromium, and nickel. There are different alloys of stainless steel made for different industrial applications. The biggest advantage of choosing stainless steel over mild steel in jewelry applications is that stainless steel will not rust, has a lovely gray color, and is quite tough. For most jewelry making purposes, it does not matter which stainless steel alloy is used.

Mild Steel

Mild steel is an alloy of iron and carbon that has less carbon than many other steel alloys. It is dark gray and will readily rust, which can be used to a jeweler's advantage. Mild steel can be drilled, formed, filed, and sawn before being tempered. It can be soldered with silver solder, although the bond is very weak. Mild steel is also produced in the form of tool steel, which can be used for making chasing, setting, and forming tools.

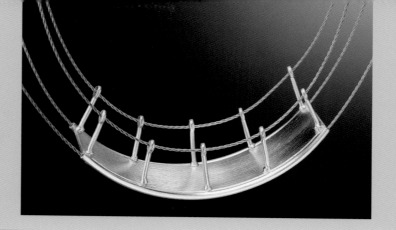

Purchasing Metals

Most nonferrous metals can be purchased in many forms, such as sheet, wire, tubing, and grain, and different suppliers offer numerous varieties of each form. For example, you can buy square tubing and rectangular tubing as well as half-round wire and rectangular wire. Buying metal in premade forms saves time and energy, and readily available materials may spur your creativity.

The Brown & Sharpe (B & S) system is most frequently used for measuring metal thickness, or *gauge*. In this system, gauges are numbered inversely; the higher the gauge number, the thinner the metal. Because each metal supplier varies slightly in its gauge measurements, the Brown & Sharpe system is best used as a guide. Consistently buying metal from the same supplier will help you maintain precise measurements. Figure 3 illustrates the relationship between Brown & Sharpe gauges and their equivalent measurements.

FIGURE 3

BROWN & SHARPE GAUGE	INCHES	MILLIMETERS
2	0.257	6.52
4	0.204	5.18
6	0.162	4.11
8	0.128	3.24
10	0.101	2.57
12	0.080	2.03
14	0.064	1.63
16	0.050	1.27
18	0.040	1.02
20	0.031	0.79
22	0.025	0.64
24	0.020	0.51
26	0.015	0.38
28	0.012	0.30
30	0.010	0.25

Tubing in assorted metals, shapes, and gauges

Wire in assorted metals and gauges

LEFT: Kristin Ivy
Ring & Reliquary, 2005. Ring, 2.5 x 2.5 x 0.6 cm. Copper, enamel, wood, sterling silver, thermoplastic, butterfly wing; hand fabricated, etched, oxidized, inlaid. Photos © Norman Watkins

FAR LEFT: Nina Mann
Ring 18KY Ruby, 2004. 1.27 cm wide. Shibuishi; amalgamated, reticulated, molded in sheet form, cast, fabricated. Photo © Ralph Gabriner

Work Hardening & Annealing

Each metal has its own crystalline structure, and when a metal is worked, its crystalline structure changes. *Work hardening* is a term that describes what occurs on a molecular level when metal has been stressed in some way, such as being hammered or bent. Work hardening makes the metal harder by pushing the atoms in its crystalline structure closer together.

Annealing is a process that reverses the effect of work hardening. When a certain amount of heat is applied to work-hardened metal, the atoms in the crystalline structure of the metal spread back apart, making the metal softer. Different metals anneal at different temperatures, and the indicator that the correct annealing temperature has been achieved is the color of the metal when heated (see figure 4). Some heated metals must be *quenched* (immediately placed into cold water) to anneal fully, while others must air cool. Most metals other than steel are heated to a dull red color, and then quenched as soon as the redness disappears. (The redness usually disappears by the time it takes to get the metal to the water with tongs.) Steel is heated to a dull red color, and then air cooled.

Metals are usually annealed after soldering. This can be a difficult step in the fabrication of some pieces, especially when there is no ready way to work harden the metal. Small wires such as earring posts can be hardened simply by using pliers and gently twisting the post. In other situations when the metal cannot be work hardened through standard means, apply the process of *age hardening*. To increase the strength of the metal using this method, place it in an oven preheated to 536°F (280°C) for 2½ hours.

FIGURE 4
Annealing Processes for Different Metals

ALLOY OR METAL	OVEN TEMPERATURE	TEMPERATURE BY COLOR (FOR TORCH ANNEALING FOLLOWED BY WATER QUENCHING)
Pure gold	400°F (204°C)	Black heat
Pure silver	400°F (204°C)	Black heat
22- &18- karat yellow gold	1000°–1100°F (538°–593°C)	Very dark red
14-karat yellow gold	1200°F (649°C)	Dark red
Sterling silver	1100°–1150°F (593°–621°C)	Barely visible red

FIGURE 5
Metal Statistics

METAL	SYMBOL	MELTING POINT	SPECIFIC GRAVITY
Gold	Au	1945°F (1063°C)	19.2
Silver	Ag	1761°F (960.5°C)	10.5
Sterling silver	925	1640°F (893°C)	10.4
Platinum	Pt	3224°F (1773°C)	21.5
Palladium	Pd	2829°F (1555°C)	12.0
Rhodium	Rh	3571°F (1966°C)	12.4
Copper	Cu	1981°F (1083°C)	8.96
Brass	70/30 Brass	1750°F (954°C)	8.5
Aluminum	Al	1220°F (660°C)	2.7
Nickel	Ni	2651°F (1453°C)	8.9
Iron	Fe	2802°F (1539°C)	7.9
Titanium	Ti	3047°F (1675°C)	4.5
Niobium	Nb	4474°F (2468°C)	8.6

Gallery
Metals & Their Properties

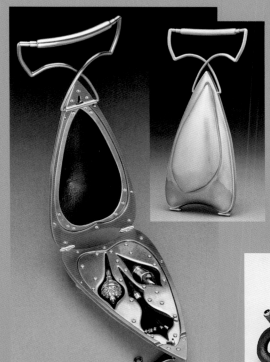

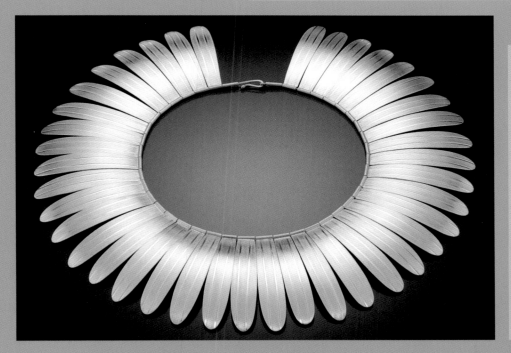

TOP LEFT: **Angela Bubash**
Implements for Enticement (handbag with three interchangeable elements), 2003. 17.8 x 6.4 x 3.8 cm. Sterling silver, copper, garnets, flowers, glass, leather, rubber, stainless steel; die formed, forged, fabricated. Photos © Tom Mills

TOP CENTER: **Roberta** and **David Williamson**
Bouquet, 1998. 11 x 3.5 x 1 cm. Sterling silver; hand fabricated, chased, textured, formed, roller printed. Photo © James Beards

TOP RIGHT: **Peg Fetter**
Snap Bracelet, 2003. 6 x 5 x 1.3 cm. Steel, 14-karat gold, diamond; forged, torched, oxidized, tube set, drilled, heat bead riveted, waxed. Photo © Don Casper

CENTER RIGHT: **Beate Eismann**
3 brooches, 2002. Largest, 7.2 x 6 x 4 cm. Aluminum, silver, various stones; die formed, anodized, set. Photo © Helga Schulze-Brinkop

BOTTOM LEFT: **Marguerite Chiang Manteau**
Love Me, Love Me Not Collar, 2004. 25.4 cm in diameter. Sterling silver, 18-karat gold; roller printed, hand fabricated. Photo © Hap Sakwa

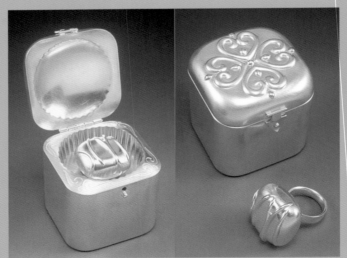

TOP: **Jason Morrissey**
Metal Beads and Links, 1999–2003.
Largest, 7 x 5 x 1.7 cm. Copper, silver,
bronze; forged. Photo © Robert Diamante

CENTER LEFT: **Rob Jackson**
Pointed Necklace (detail), 2004. 4 x 4
x 0.5 cm. Iron, steel, 18-karat gold, 22-
karat gold, ruby, diamonds; hand fabricated, bezel set. Photo © artist

CENTER RIGHT: **Ronda Coryell**
Untitled (detail), 2002. 3.5 x 5.5 cm.
22-karat gold, spinel; repoussé,
chased, granulation. Photo © George Post

BOTTOM: **Junghyun Woo**
Something Sweet, 2001. Container,
5.5 x 4.5 x 4.5 cm. 18-karat gold, sterling silver; hand fabricated, die formed,
etched. Photos © Helen Shirk

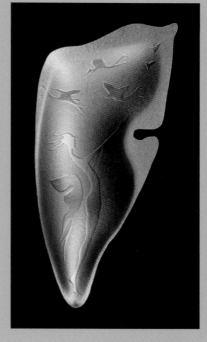

TOP: **Nancy Mēgan Corwin**
Sustainable, 2003. 1.3 x 28 cm in diameter. Sterling silver, drusy quartz; forged, oxidized. Photo © Doug Yaple

BOTTOM LEFT: **Jacqueline Myers**
22-Karat Gold Flower Earrings with Leaf Jackets, 2004. Each, 3.2 x 0.8 x 0.2 cm. 22-karat gold, 18-karat gold; hand fabricated, repoussé. Photo © Stanley J. Myers

BOTTOM CENTER: **Jacqueline Myers**
Pin/Butterfly Women, 1998. 10.2 x 4.4 x 0.6 cm. Copper; die formed with a hand-cut die, roller printed, hand fabricated. Photo © Stanley J. Myers

BOTTOM RIGHT: **Tom Ferrero**
Giraffe Earrings, 2000. Each, 7 x 2 x 2 cm. Fine gold, 18-karat gold, sterling silver, topaz, patina; hand fabricated, kum boo. Photo © Dan Neuburger

Tools & Equipment

This survey covers the most frequently used tools for making jewelry grouped by primary purpose. (Tools required for more specialized techniques are discussed in later chapters.) At the end of the glossary, all tools are condensed into two kits, a Bench Tool Kit and a Soldering Kit, to be used as a reference guide when you are learning the techniques and creating the projects in this book.

Support Surfaces

Bench Pin

A bench pin provides a sawing surface that allows you to manipulate the saw and the metal easily. Bench pins are available in many styles and sizes. For those who do not have a jeweler's bench, a portable bench pin is a good choice. It comes with a precut V slot for sawing and has a C clamp specifically designed to attach the bench pin to a tabletop. A standard bench pin for a jeweler's bench does not have a precut V slot. It must be cut out with a saw or a jigsaw. Beginning jewelers can make their own bench pin from a plain piece of smooth wood and a construction C clamp.

Bench pins and clamp

Steel Block

A steel block is an essential tool that provides even and strong support for hammering. Most steel blocks are 2 x 2 inches (5.1 x 5.1 cm) or 4 x 4 inches (10.2 x 10.2 cm). The block has a highly polished surface that should be treated with care. Any marks on the steel block will be transferred to the metal when it's hammered.

Centerpunches (left), steel blocks (right)

Anvil

An anvil is a large piece of steel with a smooth face used to support metal when it's being forged. Most anvils have a horn that can be used to bend metal or support hollow forms such as the interior of a cup.

From top: forging hammer, anvil, stump

Cutting Tools

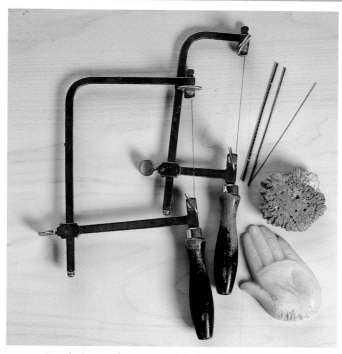

Jeweler's saw frame, saw blades, beeswax

Needle files (top), bastard files (bottom)

Needle Files

Needle files are short, usually only 6 inches (15.2 cm) in total length, and much narrower than hand files. Needle files are available in many shapes and have teeth in various grits. A basic set of needle files includes a barrette file, a half-round file, a round file, a square file, and a triangular file. A medium- to fine-cut tooth is best for beginning jewelers.

Jeweler's Saw Frame

Although there are many varieties of jeweler's saw frames, a basic frame with a wooden handle and a metal jaw is satisfactory for beginning jewelers. The most common and most practical throat sizes are 60 mm and 100 mm. Larger or smaller saw throats may be advantageous depending on the size of the metalwork.

Saw Blades

Many brands and sizes of blades for jeweler's saws are produced. Size 3 is the largest, and sizes 1/0, 2/0, and 3/0 are smaller. A good size for almost any jewelry application, even for professional jewelers, is 3/0. Always invest in high-quality blades. Less expensive blades are of inferior quality; they break more easily and are not worth the money saved. Beeswax is an effective blade lubricant that makes sawing smoother and easier.

Bastard File

A bastard file is a large hand file with coarse teeth, and can be single cut or cross cut. (Either type is appropriate for the basic filing required of this tool.) Its teeth should be coarse enough that you can feel the grit, but not so coarse that when you run your fingers over the file your fingers get caught on the teeth.

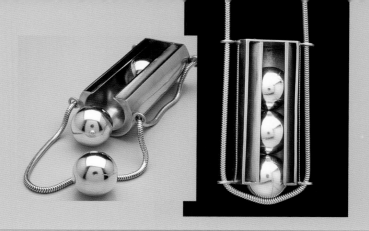

Sandpapers & Scrubbers

Abrasive papers used to sand metal are different from those for sanding wood. Their grit is attached to the paper with a stronger fixative. This bond allows the abrasive to effectively shape and finish the metal and it gives the paper a longer working life and the ability to be used both wet and dry. Metal sanding papers come in many grit sizes from coarse to fine. Higher numbered papers have finer grits. Most jewelers prefer 220-, 400-, and 600-grit papers. Use them in accordance with specific finishing tasks, gradually working with finer and finer grits if a smooth finish is desired. Green scrub pads and different grades of steel wool are also commonly used for sanding and finishing metal.

Clockwise from top: clipboard with heavy-grit emery cloth, dust mask, sandpaper strips, green scrub pad, fine-grit steel wool, heavy-grit steel wool

Hammers

Chasing Hammer

Although the chasing hammer was specifically designed for the technique of chasing, it is the most versatile hammer for jewelry making because it is appropriately weighted to give a gentle but firm blow. The head of a chasing hammer is made of polished steel and has two faces with different shapes. One face is wide, smooth, and slightly convex while the opposite face is ball-shaped.

Rawhide or Wooden Mallet

A rawhide or wooden mallet is used to form metal without distorting its surface. These large hammers have wide cylindrical heads and two flat faces.

Forging Hammer

The forging hammer is specifically weighted for moving metal. It has two smooth faces—one is round and slightly domed for planishing, and the other is rectangular and rounded for pushing and stretching metal in opposite directions to the horizontal blow.

Clockwise from left: weighted metal hammer, forging hammer, rawhide mallet, chasing hammer, rubber mallet

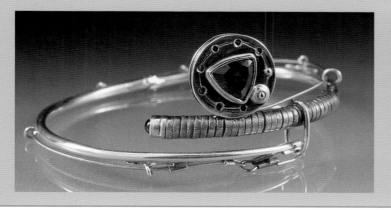

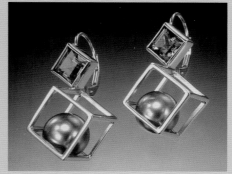

Forming Tools

Mandrel

A mandrel is a form, most often cylindrical, around which wire is wrapped or thin sheet metal is shaped or hammered. Some mandrels are tapered while others have a uniform width. Commercial mandrels specifically designed for forming rings and bracelets are available, but there are scores of other objects that can be adapted into mandrels, such as tubing, dowels, pencils, and pipes.

Dapping Block & Dapping Punches

A dapping block is a steel or wooden block with different sizes of depressions into which metal is formed. Most depressions are half spheres, but other shapes such as ovals can be custom carved into a block. The dapping punches are used to push the metal into the depressions in the block, and different size punches fit different depressions. Made of either wood or steel, the punches have one round or curved end and one flat end on which to hammer.

Steel and wood dapping blocks, forming block, and punches

Rolling Mill

This multipurpose machine has two round rollers, and the space between them is adjustable. Once the rollers are positioned with the desired setting, a long handle on the side of the machine is turned, pushing metal through the rollers to make it thinner or imprint a design. Several types of rollers are available, including ones for sheet metal that have a flat face, ones with half-round depressions for making half-round wire, and ones with square depressions for making square wire. Fancy patterned rollers for making patterned wire and sheet metal are also available.

Assorted mandrels

Rolling mill

The Flexible Shaft & Its Attachments

Flexible Shaft

A very wise investment, the flexible shaft machine is an important tool because it accepts most types of drill bits and many attachments necessary for making jewelry. The flexible shaft (or flex shaft, as it is commonly known) consists of a mounted motor and a hand piece connected by a long, flexible shaft. It comes with a foot pedal for controlling the speed of the attachment, an action similar to operating a sewing machine or the gas pedal of a car.

Drill Bits

Jeweler's drill bits are specifically designed for drilling metal, and they are made of high-carbon steel that will resist breakage. The chuck in the flexible shaft machine is sized to accommodate the smaller-than-average size of these bits. Most bits are measured by their diameter in millimeters, but some correspond to wire gauge sizes. They are sold in sets or can be purchased individually as needed.

Burrs

Different types of burrs are inserted into the end of a flexible shaft to perform different jobs, such as cutting, setting, and carving. Having a variety of burrs will make accomplishing key elements of your work easier.

Separating Disc

This round, thin disc of carborundum attaches to a mandrel and is used with the flexible shaft machine. Separating discs are cutting discs, but they can also be used for gentle carving. Wearing eye protection when using a separating disc is mandatory; the thin discs often break and can fly across a room.

Flexible shaft attachments

Clockwise from top: flexible shaft, drill bits, alternative hand pieces, chuck key, fully assembled hand piece

Small Hand Tools

Scribe

A scribe is a pointed tool used to make marks on metal. You'll use a scribe to draw points and lines or to transfer designs. You can make your own scribe by sharpening the end of a piece of scrap metal (such as a nail) or you can purchase a commercial scribe.

Assorted plastic templates, digital calipers, scribe

Stainless Steel Ruler

The precision and durability of a short stainless steel ruler is invaluable to any jeweler. This compact measuring device is easy to maneuver on small surfaces and resists damage well. Its lengths are given in small, easily divisible metric increments, such as centimeters and millimeters, as well as in inches.

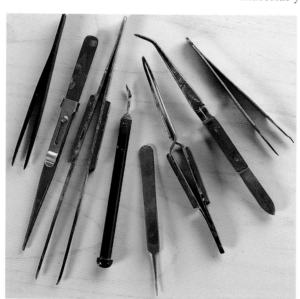

From left: tweezers, locking tweezers for stones, wooden handled tweezers, solder pick, micro-nose tweezers, straight wooden-handled cross-locking tweezers, bent wooden-handled cross-locking tweezers, tweezers

Calipers

Calipers are a precise tool for taking exact measurements. They can also be locked at a certain length to provide consistent measurements. I like using digital calipers, although some jewelers are more comfortable using analog calipers.

Tweezers

Tweezers are useful when the material you're working with is very hot or very small. A sharp set is handy for precisely placing solder paillons. Self-locking tweezers come in many designs, some with wooden heat stops on their handle.

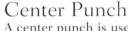

Pliers

The jaws of flat-nose pliers have flat and tapered exterior surfaces and flush interior surfaces. They are useful for holding onto objects firmly, such as one side of a jump ring. Chain-nose pliers are round on the exterior of the jaw, flat on the interior, and tapered. Use them to reach into small places. Fully rounded and tapered jaws make round-nose pliers an excellent tool for forming wire into round shapes.

Center Punch

A center punch is used to mark a point on a metal surface prior to drilling. This preliminary step helps hold the drill bit in the desired location. A center punch can be purchased or handmade by filing a nail to a sharp point (see photo, page 18).

Burnisher

A burnisher is a hand tool chiefly used to smooth metal, but it is also helpful for hand polishing or brightening small areas. It has a wooden handle and a smooth, curved metal tip that should remain highly polished (see photo, page 139).

Flaring Tool

A flaring tool is a small tapered hand tool used to flare the end of tubing when making tube rivets. There are many ways to make a flaring tool, such as filing the end of a nail into a point. The flared end of a broken burr or a small dapping punch can also work well.

Chasing & Repoussé Tools

When the top of a chasing or repoussé tool is hammered, the opposite end makes an impression in metal. Each impression shapes and patterns metal in a way that is unique to the individual tool. Commercial chasing and repoussé tools can be purchased, or you can create custom tools to suit your needs (see pages 28–30). For more information on chasing tools, see page 39.

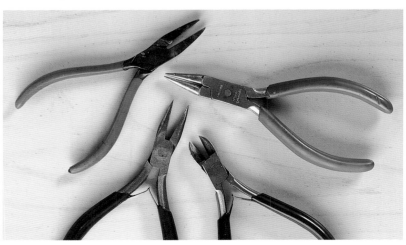

Clockwise from top: flat-nose pliers, round-nose pliers, snips, needle-nose pliers

FAR LEFT: **Joanna Gollberg**
Howard, 2001. 15.2 x 5.1 x 0.3 cm. Sterling silver, nickel silver, brass, copper, rubies, horsehair; marriage of metal, fabricated. Photo © keithwright.com

LEFT: **Darren Fisher**
Untitled, 2002. 4.5 x 46 cm. Shibuishi, copper, sterling silver, patina; forged, fabricated. Photo © artist

RIGHT: **Masumi Kataoka**
Locked Time, 2000. 4 x 8 x 18 cm. Sterling silver, brass, vinyl, human hair. Photo © Chris Irick

Soldering Tools & Materials

Soldering Torch

To solder you must have heat, and this heat is most often produced by a flame. This flame comes from a torch where a gas and either air or oxygen combine and are lit. The most easily accessible and reasonably priced gas to use for soldering is propane, although acetylene, which burns hotter than propane, is also very popular. Two separate tanks, one for the gas and one for the oxygen, are required. Each is fitted with a regulator used to set and maintain pressure and gas flow. Individual hoses, color-coded for safety, are attached to the regulators and run to the torch handle. A tip is attached to the handle to shape the size of the flame.

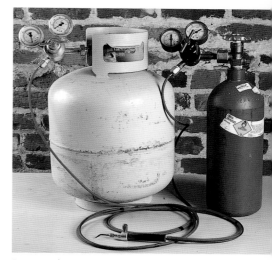

Propane/oxygen tanks with fittings

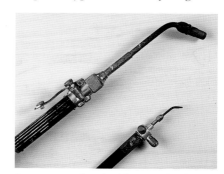

Large annealing/welding tip (top), mini tip (bottom)

Oxygen/acetylene tanks with fittings

Torch hand piece and tip (top), striker (bottom)

Tank regulators and gauges

Soldering Surfaces

Soldering must be done on top of a surface that is heat-resistant. You can create this surface with a firebrick, a variety of ceramic blocks, or a charcoal block.

Soldering Flux

Solder flows only on a clean metal surface. If oxygen reaches the surface of the metal when it is heated, oxides form. Flux is a substance that promotes the joining of metals by forming a layer that blocks the oxygen. Before soldering, apply flux to the surfaces to be joined to facilitate their union. Different types of flux are effective at different heat levels, most commonly between 1100° and 1500°F (600° and 800°C). Be sure to use the flux that corresponds to your soldering temperature.

Striker

A striker is a tool that creates a spark by rubbing a flint against a piece of steel.

Solder

Solder is a metal alloy that, when melted, joins metallic surfaces. Different types of metal and different processes require the use of different solders. Gold and silver solders, alloyed to a lower melting temperature than the metals they join, are the most

From left: paste solder, powdered solder, wire solder, sheet solder

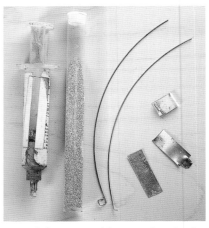

Wire solder indicators, from top: hard, medium, easy

Clockwise from left: honeycomb soldering block, rotating dish with ceramic media, ceramic block, firebrick, compressed charcoal block

From left: flux brush, flux container with small tip, spray bottle, paste flux, liquid flux

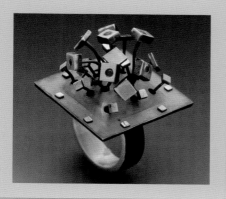  

common. Within these two main categories there are several varieties of solder based on the temperature at which they melt and flow. For silver solders, the most common are extra easy, easy, medium, hard, and IT (listed in order of increasing flow point). Gold solders are identified by their karat (generally 10, 14, or 16). Lower karat gold solders have lower melting temperatures than higher karat gold solders. The flow points of gold solders may vary from manufacturer to manufacturer, so when placing your order, request a data sheet from your supplier. Solder is sold in several forms, the most popular being wire and sheet. Choose the type you like best for the soldering method being used.

Pickle

Pickle is an acidic compound that removes flux and oxidized surfaces from soldered metal. Many varieties can be used, the most common being sodium bisulphate. This chemical is available from jewelry suppliers. Nontoxic substitutes include alum or a solution of vinegar and salt. To obtain the fastest results, use pickle that's been heated in a slow cooker dedicated to this process.

Tool Kits

Rest assured that not every project calls for every tool on these lists. I recommend that you first read the instructions completely, and then assemble the required tools.

Bench Tool Kit

Bench pin
Steel block
Anvil
Jeweler's saw frame
Saw blades
Beeswax
Needle files
Bastard file
220- and 400-grit sandpaper
Chasing hammer
Rawhide or wooden mallet
Forging hammer
Mandrels
Dapping block and punches
Rolling mill
Flexible shaft
Wood block
Drill bits
Burrs
Separating disc
Scribe
Stainless steel ruler
Calipers
Pliers
Center punch
Flaring tool
Chasing and repoussé tools
Burnisher
Safety glasses
Safety gloves
Hearing protection
Dust mask

Soldering Kit

Soldering torch
Striker
Heat-resistant soldering surfaces, such as charcoal blocks, firebricks, or ceramic plates
Flux
Flux brush or other applicator
Hard, medium, and easy solder
Snips for cutting wire solder
Small embroidery scissors for cutting sheet solder
Solder pick
Tweezers
Cross-locking tweezers with wooden handle
Copper tongs
Water for quenching
Pickle
Pickle warming pot, such as a slow cooker
Safety glasses
Fire extinguisher

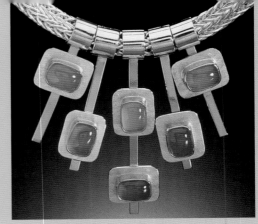

Safety Equipment

Hearing Protection

To protect your hearing, especially while forging, use a headset with large padded ear coverings or rubber earplugs.

Eye Protection

Wearing safety glasses is an important precaution to take when using any machine. I recommend you wear them every time you work with the flexible shaft and when you solder.

Lung Protection

To protect your lungs from particle inhalation, wear a disposable dust mask when sanding and polishing metal or using powdered enamels. A respirator is not essential unless you work with niello, which contains lead.

Skin Protection

Wear safety gloves when polishing to protect your fingers from heat and when using chemicals to etch or patina metal. Small gloves and green protective tape can also protect your skin during sanding.

Making Chasing Tools

Once you know how to make chasing tools, you can create an infinite variety of stamps and liners for patterning and moving metal.

MATERIALS

Standard water-quenching tool steel, any size, round or square profile
Tripoli, bobbing, and rouge polishing compounds

TOOLS & SUPPLIES

Bench tool kit, page 27
Steel burrs (optional)
Flexible-shaft polishing accessories
Soldering kit, page 27
Heavy pliers (optional)

STEP BY STEP

1 Using the jeweler's saw, cut a length of tool steel between 3 and 4 inches (7.6 and 10.2 cm) long. (Some jewelers prefer using shorter chasing tools that are approximately 2 inches [5.1 cm] long. This is a matter of personal preference, so I encourage you to experiment and find the length that best suits you.)

2 Use files to carve a design or shape into one end of the tool steel. Since tool steel is pre-annealed, carving should be easy, but it may take a long time to achieve the desired design. Use steel burrs as needed to help carve your design. (For example, to make an O shape you would carve the outer shape of the O with a needle file, and then remove the metal in the middle of the O with a round burr.)

3 Sand the carved design to a 400-grit finish, and then polish it to a rouge shine (see pages 56 and 57 for polishing instructions). Polishing the end helps the chasing tool glide through the metal.

4 Light the torch, adjust the flame, and heat the carved end of the chasing tool. (You may need to hold the tool in a pair of heavy pliers to keep from burning your fingers.) Don't heat the entire tool, just the tip. When it becomes red-orange hot, immediately quench the whole tool in water until it is cool. This hardens the steel and makes it brittle. Dry the tool.

5 Reheat the tip of the chasing tool until you see a bit of blue and a bit of a cornhusk yellow color on the steel (see photo). Once these colors appear, immediately quench the tool. This step *tempers* the steel, meaning that the brittleness of the metal has been removed and the tool is now hard enough to retain its design through repeated hammering.

6 Repeat steps 4 and 5 on the opposite end of the tool, the end that will be hammered.

7 Repolish the carved end of the tool to a rouge shine.

BENCH TIP

You can use this hardening and tempering procedure to alter any chasing tools you already have. This way, you can make a tool you need from ones that aren't working right for you. The tool may need annealing before it can be carved. To do this, heat the tool to a dull red color and let it air cool.

Variations: Decorative Chasing Tools

Giving handmade chasing tools attractive flourishes, such as unique twists and carvings, makes them easy to identify and deeply satisfying to use. The materials, tools, and supplies you will need to make a twisted square tool are the same as those listed for Making Chasing Tools on page 28 with the addition of a vise.

Twisted Square Tool

STEP BY STEP

1 Carve the end of the tool into the desired shape. Place the tool in a vise so that it is perpendicular to the jaws of the vise.

2 Heat the entire tool with the torch until it is red hot. While it is red hot, grasp the tool with heavy pliers and begin twisting. (You may need someone else to hold the torch when you do this. Because the metal will only move when it is red hot, heat must be constantly applied.) As

you twist, keep the tool in a straight line, perpendicular to the jaws of the vise. Option: To make a fancy twist, twist the steel in one direction and then back in the other direction.

3 After twisting, let the chasing tool cool, and then harden and temper its ends.

New Tool *A vise is a clamping device that holds a piece of metal in position. The two jaws of the vise are closed or opened by a screw or lever.*

Carved Round Tool

When using round tool steel stock, you can carve decorative designs on the shaft of the tool with needle files. It is well worth the time and effort it takes to decorate a tool. The pleasure you'll get from using it is immense.

Gallery

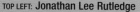

TOP LEFT: **Jonathan Lee Rutledge**
Untitled, 2004. Pendant, 3.3 cm; strand, 43 cm long. 22-karat gold, rhodolite garnet, pearl; fused, granulation, hand fabricated. Photo © Hap Sakwa

TOP CENTER: **Ken Thibado**
She Belongs to Me, 2005. 6.6 x 2.8 x 0.5 cm. Sterling silver, 14-karat gold, diamonds, found objects, resin; hand fabricated, tube set, bezel set. Photo © Robert Diamante

TOP RIGHT: **Angela Bubash**
Lust Pomander (detail), 2003. 25.4 x 11.4 x 0.6 cm. Sterling silver, garnet, damiana, vetiver, jasmine; forged, fabricated, cast. Photo © Tom Mills

BOTTOM RIGHT: **Tom Ferrero**
The Virgin Tea Infuser, 2002. 17 x 5 x 5 cm. 22-karat gold, sterling silver, pyrope garnet, amethyst; hand fabricated, chased, repoussé, marriage of metal, raised, cast, set, granulation. Photos © Dan Neuburger

Gallery

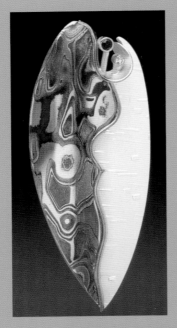

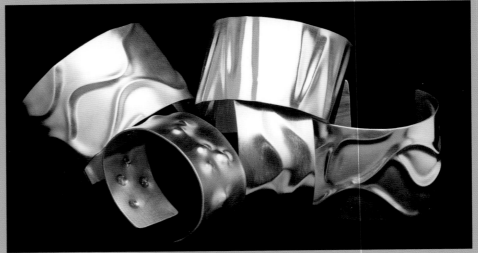

TOP LEFT: **Joan Tenenbaum**
Tidelands Brooch II, 2000. 5.6 x 2.2 x 1.3 cm. 18-karat gold, sterling silver, 22-karat gold, sapphire, diamond; mokume gane, etched, roller printed, hand fabricated, oxidized, riveted. Photo © Doug Yaple

TOP CENTER: **Joanna Gollberg**
Hair Sticks, 2001. Each, 15.2 x 3.2 x 1.3 cm. Sterling silver, 14-karat gold, nickel silver, copper; marriage of metal, hollow formed, fabricated. Photo © keithwright.com

TOP RIGHT: **Nancy E. Fleming**
Die Formed, 2003. 7.6 x 5.1 cm. Sterling silver, 14-karat gold; die formed, kum boo, roller printed. Photo © Seth Tice-Lewis. Courtesy of Ariel Gallery, Asheville, North Carolina

CENTER LEFT: **Taweesak Molsawat**
Kommara (The Prison of the Self), 2000. 5 x 1.9 x 2.3 cm. Sterling silver, copper, bronze; etched, cast, hand fabricated, oxidized. Photo © artist

CENTER RIGHT: **Ericia Bartels-Dawkins**
Various Hydraulic Cuffs, 2002. Each, 5 x 10 x 7.5 cm. Sterling silver; hydraulic formed. Photo © Brent Bacher

BOTTOM LEFT: **Erica Stankwytch Bailey**
Composite, 2004. 60 x 60 x 3 cm. Sterling silver, copper, pearl; dapped, hollow form constructed, marriage of metal, roller printed, pierced. Photo © Joe Lechleider

Metalworking Basics

Some jewelry-making skills are practiced no matter how experienced you are. These include cold and hot techniques. At the end of this chapter, on pages 60–63, you will find two projects that will allow you to use metalworking basics, such as sawing, piercing, riveting, chasing, and finishing.

Cold Techniques

The following techniques alter the surface of metal without the use of heat. They are fundamental skills every jeweler should know, and most can be accomplished with standard bench tools.

Cleaning Metal

It is essential that you know how to clean a metal sheet. Several techniques, such as soldering, enameling, and kum boo, require a metal surface that is completely clean.

MATERIALS
Scrap or inexpensive sheet metal
Pumice or household cleanser (optional)

TOOLS & SUPPLIES
Soft brush, green scrub pad, sandpaper, or steel wool

STEP BY STEP

1 Hold the metal sheet by its edges to avoid depositing finger grease. Scrub the metal surface with pumice or a household abrasive cleanser as shown in photo A. Alternately, you can use a green scrub pad (photo B), sandpaper, a brass brush (photo C), or steel wool.

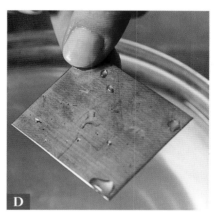

2 Thoroughly rinse the metal. If water beads up on the metal after it has been cleaned (photo D), then oil and/or dirt are still present. If water sheets off the metal (photo E), then the metal is completely clean.

Transferring a Design

Once a design is drawn on paper, it can be transferred onto sheet metal. This simple process provides clear guidelines to follow with a jeweler's saw. When transferring any design, conserve as much surface space on the metal as possible. Avoid starting a design in the center of a metal sheet; instead, place the design near an edge or a corner. Often, the straight lines of the sheet metal edges can be used to reduce the amount of sawing needed. Metal rulers and plastic templates can be used with the scribe to transfer geometric designs. If a design is more intricate or has a looser, more organic form, it's best to use graphite transfer paper.

Using Graphite Transfer Paper

MATERIALS
Sheet metal of your choice

TOOLS & SUPPLIES
Pencil and paper or pattern to
    photocopy
Graphite transfer paper
Tape
Scribe

STEP BY STEP

1 Draw an original design on paper or photocopy a pattern.

2 With the graphite-coated side facing down, insert a piece of transfer paper between the design and the sheet metal. Tape the design to the metal so it stays in place.

3 Firmly trace over the design with a pencil or scribe. Remove the graphite transfer paper and the design.

4 Use the scribe to trace back over the transferred lines so the design won't rub off the metal.

Sawing & Piercing

Sawing and piercing are two fundamental metalworking skills. They can be used for cutting out simple shapes or creating complex patterns.

Sawing Posture

Sawing near eye level makes it easier to see what you are doing and reduces physical problems such as backaches. For these reasons, most jeweler's benches are approximately 1 foot (30.5 cm) taller than standard tables. If you plan to saw at a table of normal height, use a short stool. This is not just for convenience—working with an incorrect body position can cause serious back problems over time. To further protect your body, keep a straight back while sawing.

BENCH TIP

A blade that is too tight or too loose in the frame can break quite easily, and if the blade is too loose, your sawing will not progress well.

Installing a Saw Blade into a Jeweler's Saw Frame
STEP BY STEP

1 Open the jaw of the saw frame approximately 10 mm longer than the length of the saw blade.

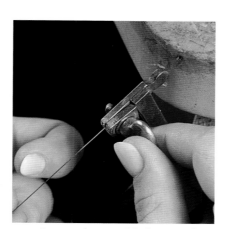

2 Insert the saw blade into the top nut of the saw frame with the teeth of the blade facing toward you and pointing down. Tighten the nut.

3 With the saw blade facing up, rest the end of the saw frame handle on your sternum, and rest the top edge of the saw frame against the jeweler's bench or worktable.

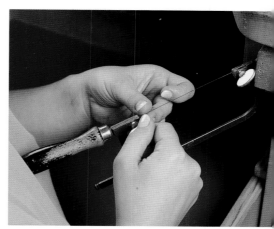

4 Using your sternum, push the saw handle forward to slightly shorten the length of the saw frame jaw. With the jaw length shortened, place the end of the saw blade into the lower nut, then tighten. Release the pressure on the saw frame. The saw blade should be quite taut in the frame, and if you pluck the blade like a musical instrument string, it should make a nice pinging sound.

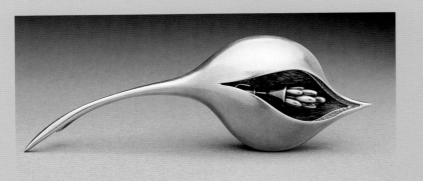

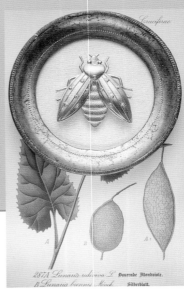

Sawing Metal

MATERIALS

Scrap or inexpensive sheet metal

TOOLS & SUPPLIES

Bench tool kit, page 27

STEP BY STEP

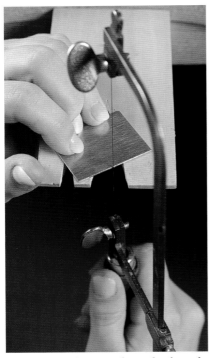

1 Place the metal on the bench pin. Using an upward stroke, make one quick run up the metal edge with the saw blade. This creates a small indention on the metal edge where the saw teeth can bite.

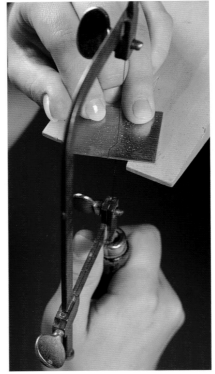

2 Position the top of the saw blade on the indention and move the saw frame up and down, letting the saw teeth do all the work on the downward stroke. Keep the saw at a 90-degree angle to the metal being cut, and point the frame forward at all times, unless you're turning a sharp corner.

BENCH TIPS

Select the correct saw frame for the size of the metal being cut.

Hold the saw handle lightly in your hand rather than gripping it tightly.

Run the saw blade against a block of beeswax prior to sawing to increase the smoothness of the stroke and decrease the rough bite of the blade.

Turn the metal, not the saw frame, when rounding a corner or sawing an arc.

To turn a sharp corner, simultaneously and quickly turn the metal and the saw while continuing to move the saw up and down.

Practice. Practice. And practice some more. When learning to saw, beginners often break a lot of blades. No need to fret if this happens to you—over time you'll become quite proficient.

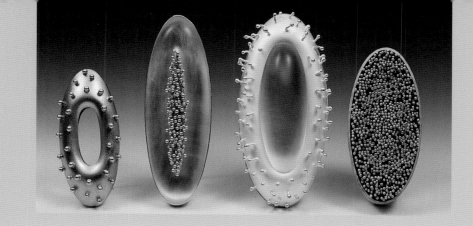

Drilling & Piercing Metal

MATERIALS
Scrap or inexpensive sheet metal

TOOLS & SUPPLIES
Bench tool kit, page 27

STEP BY STEP

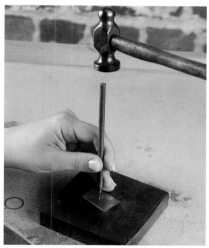

1 Determine where to drill the hole in the metal. Place the steel block on your jeweler's bench or worktable and rest the metal on the steel block. Place the tip of the center punch on the location to be drilled. As shown in the photo, tap the top of the center punch with the chasing hammer to lightly indent, or *dimple*, the metal. (The dimple guides the drill bit, ensuring that the hole is made precisely in the desired location. If this indentation is not made, the bit can swerve over the metal surface, making marks that will have to be sanded off later.)

2 Place the wood block on your jeweler's bench or worktable and place the dimpled metal on the block. (You may want to make this block a designated drilling surface.) Secure the drill bit in the flexible shaft and position the tip of the bit on the dimple. Drill the hole with the flexible shaft, using an even, medium speed and keeping the drill bit at a 90-degree angle to the metal.

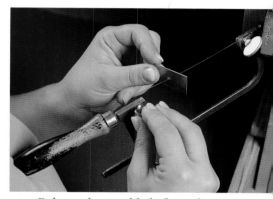

3 Release the saw blade from the bottom nut of the frame and thread the loose end through the drilled hole (see photo). Reattach the blade to the frame, tightening the nut. (To accomplish this with two hands, rest the end of the handle against your sternum and the top of the frame against the bench while holding the metal in one hand and tightening the nut with the other.) Saw out the interior shapes following standard sawing procedures.

4 Release the end of the saw blade from the bottom nut of the frame and slide off the pierced metal. Reattach the blade to the frame, and tighten the nut.

BENCH TIPS

Maintain a medium flexible shaft speed when drilling; the motor should never be racing or creeping along.

When drilling thicker metals, dip the bit into beeswax or 3-in-1 oil before drilling each hole.

Keep the drill bit at a 90-degree angle to the metal, or it may break.

If a drill bit breaks and gets stuck in the metal, soak it overnight in a solution of alum and water. This helps dissolve the broken bit, making it easier to remove.

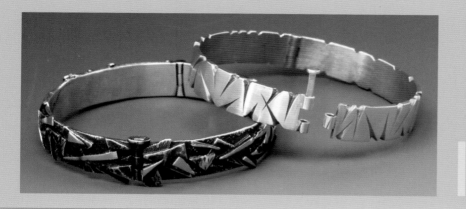

Filing Metal

After sawing, you will often need to file the cut metal. Filing cleans up uneven lines by removing metal in specific areas. Normally, all the teeth on a file are pointed in one direction and metal is removed only on the forward stroke. On the backward stroke, the file will not remove metal but it will scratch the surface, falsely giving the appearance that metal has been removed.

MATERIALS

Scrap or inexpensive sheet metal

TOOLS & SUPPLIES

Bench pin
Bastard file
Assorted needle files

STEP BY STEP

1 Rest the metal to be filed against the bench pin. Select the correct file shape and coarseness for the metal.

2 Place your index finger on the top of the file. Using a firm, even stroke, move the file forward up the edge of the metal. Lift the file off the metal and reposition it for another stroke.

BENCH TIP

A file's cut size can range from very coarse to very fine. Choose a medium-cut file for general use, and for more specific purposes use a coarse- or fine-cut file. (The coarser the file, the more quickly metal is removed.)

Carving Metal

You can carve metal directly and use this technique to create a surface decoration or a relief design. The best tools for carving metal are jeweler's needle files and some flexible shaft accessories. For complex carvings, it is better to sculpt a piece out of wax and cast it in metal.

Carving with Needle Files

Draw the design to be carved on the metal or simply mark the places where carving is to be added. Choose the best needle file to make the desired shape. (For example, select a square needle file for carving square indentions or a half-round or round needle file for curved indentions.) Practice carving metal with assorted needle files to see what shapes and forms you can make. I often begin carving with one type of file, and then go back over the carved area with the barrette file to smooth the marks and make them uniform and continuous. Remember that files remove metal only on the forward stroke.

Carving with Burrs

Using burrs in the flexible shaft is necessary when you're carving within the framework of the metal rather than on an outside edge. Burrs remove metal faster than files do and may initially be necessary for removing a lot of metal quickly. Make sure these burrs are designed for use with metal, not wax. When used on metal, wax burrs will wear out quickly. After using burrs, needle files can be used to smooth out carved areas.

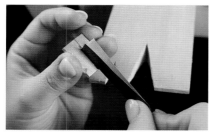

Finishing Carved Metal

Use 220- and 400-grit sandpaper to smooth the carved forms. Often, you will have to sand the metal by hand to get into hard-to-reach places. Covering a needle file with a piece of sandpaper may help you gain access.

Chasing Metal

In the technique of chasing, steel hand tools are used with a chasing hammer to make imprints in metal. The results of chasing can appear similar to that of engraving, but the processes differ substantially. Engraving actually removes part of the metal surface, while chasing simply relocates it. Chasing is an excellent form of jewelry embellishment. Designs can feature chasing as the central focus, or chasing can be used sparingly for extra interest or texture.

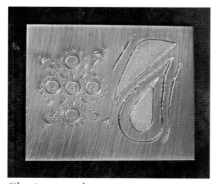

Chasing samples

Chasing Tools

Chasing tools are made from tool steel, usually round or square stock, and can be of infinite variety. The end of the tool is carved with a shape or a texture, and then the steel is hardened and tempered to make the carved design permanent. Some chasing tools are called stamps (photo A). The

design on the bottom of these tools is imprinted on the metal through the force of a hammer blow. There are also matting tools, which, when hammered, leave texture on the metal instead of a particular line design (photo B). A liner tool makes lines and curves on a metal surface and can be used to create intricate linear forms and designs (photo C). This chasing tool makes marks that are most similar to those of engraving.

Chasing a Shape or Texture

MATERIALS
Sheet metal of your choice

TOOLS & SUPPLIES
Steel block
Masking tape (optional)
Chasing tool or tools of your choice
Chasing hammer
Wooden or rawhide mallet

STEP BY STEP

1 Place the sheet metal on the steel block. (Because it provides resistance to the hammer blows, a steel block is essential to this process. Otherwise, the metal can become deformed and the stamp or chasing tool won't be able to work properly.) If desired, tape the metal to the steel block to secure it. Some jewelers prefer to perform extensive chasing in pitch. (Refer to page 76 for further instructions on working with pitch.)

2 Position the chasing tool on the metal and hold it in your fingers. Use the chasing hammer to tap the top of the tool lightly and make an impression on the sheet. (If desired, experiment on a piece of scrap sheet. Make light and hard hammer blows and examine the different marks they make.)

3 A chased metal sheet may become slightly domed because the metal molecules have been moved. The metal is thinner where the chased impressions have been made, forcing molecules toward unchased areas. To flatten the metal, turn over the sheet on the steel block so the chasing faces down. Lightly hammer the surface with a wooden or rawhide mallet to reshape the metal without leaving hammer marks. This step may need to be repeated several times during one chasing session.

Chasing a Continuous Line

MATERIALS
Sheet metal of your choice

TOOLS & SUPPLIES
Steel block
Masking tape (optional)
Liner tool
Chasing hammer
Wooden or rawhide mallet, if needed

STEP BY STEP

1 Place the sheet metal on the steel block, and tape down the metal to secure it.

2 Barely rest the liner tool on the metal and hold it in your fingers. (You will use your thumb and middle finger to guide the tool.)

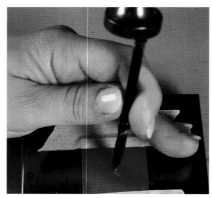

3 While making gentle blows with the chasing hammer, move the liner tool along the line to be chased, working toward your body. Do not pick up the liner tool between blows. Hold the tool

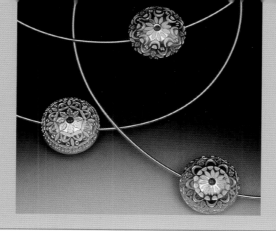

steady and make continuous and fairly rapid hammer blows. The indented line should appear smooth, not choppy. If you take a break, make sure you resume chasing with the liner tool resting near the end of the last mark made, otherwise the line will appear broken.

4 When chasing a line, if the metal becomes domed or misshapen and you are not feeling the resistance of the steel block, follow step 3 of Chasing a Shape or Texture.

BENCH TIPS

When using commercial stamps, multiple hammer blows are required to imprint the metal. To transfer the whole design, make firm taps with the hammer while rocking the stamp back and forth.

A straight liner tool is satisfactory for chasing loose curves. However, for chasing tighter curves you may need a curved liner tool. With practice, you can create a continuous line while switching back and forth between straight and curved lining tools.

Cold Connections

Cold connecting is the act of joining metal elements together without using heat. This method allows for the connection of ferrous and non-ferrous metals and for the inclusion of found objects that cannot take heat. Cold connections can be purely functional, purely decorative, or a combination of both. The primary type of cold connection used in making jewelry is riveting.

A functional rivet securely traps two or more pieces of metal together or joins some other object to metal. It passes through layers of material and is flared on each side. The three types of rivets—wire, tube, and split—function the same, but look different. Rivets can also be wonderful decorative accents without having an actual mechanical function.

Wire Riveting

MATERIALS
Sheet metal of your choice
Round wire for rivet,
    14 to 18 gauge

TOOLS & SUPPLIES
Digital calipers
Bench tool kit, page 27

STEP BY STEP

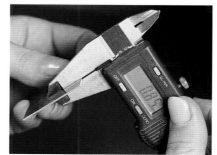

1 Use the digital calipers to measure the thickness of the sheet metal to be riveted.

2 Decide where you want to place the rivet. Dimple the metal at this point, and then drill a hole through it using a bit that is the same diameter as the round rivet wire.

3 Use the jeweler's saw to cut a length of rivet wire that is approximately 2 mm longer than the thickness of the sheet metal.

4 Hold the cut wire in the flat-nose pliers and sand the ends with 400-grit paper to remove burrs.

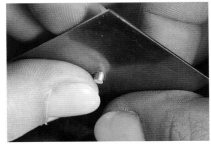

5 Thread the rivet wire though the hole drilled in step 2.

6 Place the threaded metal on top of the steel block. Use the chasing hammer to gently tap one end of the rivet wire two or three times.

7 Turn over the threaded metal. Adjust the length of

the rivet wire so an equal amount extends beyond each side of the hole. Make two or three gentle taps on the rivet wire and turn the piece over again.

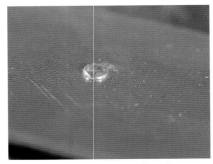

8 Repeat turning, adjusting, and tapping the wire until the ends "mushroom," forming the completed rivet.

TROUBLESHOOTING

If the wire bends before the rivet is complete, you may have cut the rivet wire too long. The other possibility is that you didn't turn the metal over enough times to rivet the wire in equal amounts. It is essential to keep turning the piece over and flaring the ends in equal amounts. You cannot completely flare one wire end and then turn the piece over and flare the other end.

BENCH TIPS

Practice makes perfect.
You'll quickly gain control
of your rivets by precisely
and repeatedly following
the step-by-step instruc-
tions and tips.

When making a rivet for the
first time, drill a hole
through only one layer of
metal and use thick 14- or
16-gauge wire. Practice riveting several times with
thick wire, and then move
on to smaller gauges. Never
make rivets with wire that is
thinner than 20 gauge; it
simply isn't strong enough.

Always use the jeweler's saw
to cut the wire into rivet
lengths. Never cut it with
snips, because they leave an
uneven end on the cut wire.

To make a completed wire
rivet head rounder and more
uniform in appearance, use a
cup burr attachment on the
flexible shaft. Cup burrs have
teeth on the inside of the cup
and can be purchased from a
jewelry tool supplier.

Tube Riveting

MATERIALS
Sheet metal of your choice
Metal tubing, 3- to 4-mm outside
diameter (OD) and other sizes
for practice

TOOLS & SUPPLIES
Digital calipers
Bench tool kit, page 27

STEP BY STEP

1 Use the digital calipers to
measure the thickness of the
sheet metal to be riveted.

2 Decide where you want to
place the rivet. Dimple the
metal at this point, and then drill
a hole through it using a bit that is
the same diameter as the tubing.

3 Use the jeweler's saw to cut a
length of tubing that is
approximately 3 mm longer than
the thickness of the sheet metal.

4 Sand the cut ends of the tubing with 400-grit sandpaper.
Thread the tubing through the
hole drilled in step 2.

5 Place the threaded sheet
metal on the steel block.
Insert the flaring tool into one end
of the tubing and make one light
tap on the flaring tool with the
chasing hammer.

6 Turn over the threaded sheet
metal. Insert the flaring tool
into the end of the tubing, and
make one light tap with the chasing hammer.

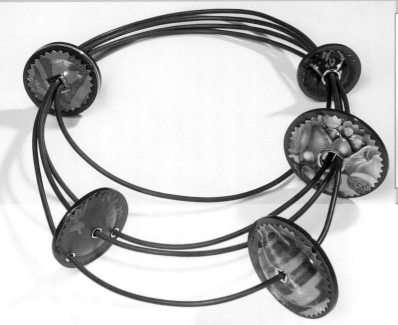

Pre-Flaring Tube Rivets

When tube riveting in hard-to-reach places, I suggest pre-flaring one side of the tube (see photo). This simple process makes your work much easier.

1 Place one cut and sanded end of a tube on the steel block. Using the flaring tool and a chasing hammer, gently tap the end of the tube to create a nice flare. (Do not to tap too hard or you'll compress the tube end resting on the steel block.)

2 Feed the tube into the rivet hole with the pre-flared end in the location that is difficult to reach. Hold some type of resistant surface against the pre-flared end of the rivet. Tap the exposed tube end with the chasing hammer; the force of the blows will secure both sides of the rivet.

7 Using the flaring tool and the chasing hammer, continue to make one tap at a time on each end of the tubing until it can't be removed from the drilled hole. Before hammering, always adjust the length of the tubing so an equal amount extends beyond each side of the hole.

8 Continue to flare the tubing by making gentle taps directly on the tubing with the ball side of the chasing hammer. (The flaring tool is no longer needed.) Regularly turn over the sheet metal to tap an equal amount on both ends of the tube. Tap the tubing until the rivet is secure.

BENCH TIPS

Practice, practice, practice. The more tube rivets you make, the more skillful you will become.

Begin making tube rivets with tubing that has an outside diameter (OD) of 3 to 4 mm, and then rivet larger and smaller tubing to feel how different sizes respond to the flaring tool and to the chasing hammer.

Making Multiple Rivets on a Circle

Riveting diagonally across the circumference of a circle helps secure the metal pieces in the proper position. When making multiple rivets in this formation, I recommend using the "clock method." Make the first rivet at 12 o'clock, the second at 6 o'clock, the third at 9 o'clock, and the fourth at 3 o'clock. To make sure the holes line up perfectly, drill and rivet at 12 o'clock and 6 o'clock, and then drill and rivet at 9 o'clock and 3 o'clock. (If more than four rivets are needed, continue making them in this formation.)

Making Multiple Rivets on a Square or Rectangle

When creating multiple rivets on a square or rectangle, begin with one corner (the upper right, for instance) and then rivet the opposite corner (the lower left in this case). Rivet a third corner that is horizontal to the first rivet (upper left), and then finish with the remaining corner (lower right). To add additional rivets for decorative purposes, it is best to drill the holes after making sure the functional rivets are holding the metal in place. That way, you will be certain the holes in both metal sheets line up.

Split Rivets

Split rivets can be made from wire or tubing. The ends of the rivet are cut with slots, the rivet is threaded through the metal to be joined, and then the slotted ends are manually flared. When making a wire split rivet, use wire that is thicker than 14 gauge or it will be difficult to cut the ends. Similarly, it is best to use tubing that is larger than 3-mm OD.

MATERIALS

> Sheet metal of your choice
> Metal tubing (larger than 3-mm OD) or wire (thicker than 14 gauge)

TOOLS & SUPPLIES

> Digital calipers
> Bench tool kit, page 27
> Parallel pliers, ring clamp, or 45/90-degree miter jig

STEP BY STEP

1 Use the digital calipers to measure the thickness of the sheet metal to be riveted.

2 Use the jeweler's saw to cut a length of tubing or wire that is at least 3 mm longer than the width of the metal. (You can use longer ends on a split rivet for decorative purposes. Experiment with different lengths to discover the possibilities. Also, both ends do not have to be slotted to the same length as long as both ends are long enough to make a secure rivet.)

3 The wire or tube must be held tightly in order to make a clean cut with the saw. Options include holding the wire or tubing with parallel pliers, holding it tightly in your fingers if it is long enough, securing the wire or tubing in a ring clamp, or fastening it in a 45/90-degree miter jig. Determine which of these methods works best for you and secure the wire or tubing.

4 Use the jeweler's saw to cut slots in both ends of the wire or tubing. Leave as much unslotted space as the thickness of the objects to be riveted. I suggest beginners start by making four slots, but you can cut as many as you like. Work with care, as it can be tricky to cut straight lines. If you choose to cut the slots with a separating disc, make sure you wear safety glasses.

5 Decide where to place the rivet, dimple the metal, and drill a hole the same diameter as the wire or tubing.

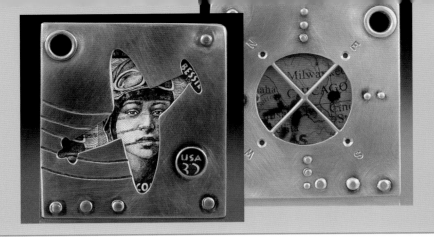

6 Begin flaring one slotted end of the wire or tubing with your fingers. If you cannot bend back the metal with your hands, use flat- or chain-nose pliers (see photo). Insert the rivet into the drilled hole. Bend all the slots on both ends of the rivet against the sheet metal. The resulting connection has a shape like an open flower.

7 To secure the flared rivets firmly, hammer them with the ball side of the chasing hammer. (Some objects being riveted will not withstand the force of a hammer blow. Use your judgment and omit this step if needed.) Sand the split rivet with 400-grit sandpaper to remove all burrs.

Riveting with Spacers

Through the use of spacers, two sheets of metal or other objects can be riveted together with a gap left between them. These spacers can be pieces of telescoping tubing, a jump ring that fits securely around a rivet, or a decorative piece of sheet metal. Spacers can move freely in a piece of jewelry, or they can be quite tight between riveted objects. Using spacers can add dimension, movement, and creativity.

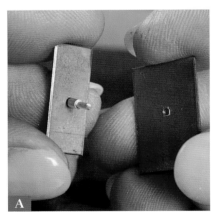

Select a spacer and slip it between the pieces being joined (photo A). The spacer must fit onto the wire or tubing exactly. If the inside diameter (ID) of the spacer is too large for the outside diameter (OD) of the wire or tube rivet, it can bend and will not have sufficient support for the required hammering.

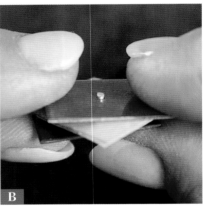

To make a moving spacer, place a thin sheet of cardboard on top of the spacer before adding the final layer of the material to be riveted (photo B). The cardboard is an extra support during the riveting process and, once detached, enables the spacer to move. Once the rivet is complete, remove the cardboard by ripping it out or by soaking the piece in water.

FAR LEFT: **Rob Jackson**
Homage to Bessie Coleman, 2000. 5 x 5 x 0.5 cm. Brass, copper, stamp, mica, map; pierced, riveted, chased. Photos © artist

LEFT: **Michael T. Gleason**
Why the Woodpecker Has a Long Beak, 2001. 6.5 x 6 x 1.5 cm. Sterling silver, titanium, plastic, paintbrush; fabricated, riveted. Photo © Don Casper

RIGHT: **Nancy Bonnema**
Rumpelstiltskin, 2004. 7.6 cm in diameter. Sterling silver, enamel, 18-karat gold, 24-karat gold. Photo © Doug Yaple

Hot Techniques

The following techniques use the heat of a torch to alter the malleability of a piece of metal (annealing) and to join two pieces of metal permanently (soldering). Most of these practices can be accomplished using the basic Soldering Kit on page 27.

Lighting an Oxyacetylene or Oxy Propane Torch

1 Check that the pressure on both gas tanks is between 5 and 10 psi (34.5 and 69 kPa). Turn the knob on the acetylene or propane gas regulator counterclockwise (left), approximately one-eighth of a turn.

2 Light the gas with the striker.

3 Turn the oxygen regulator knob slightly counterclockwise (left) to introduce a trace of oxygen into the flame. Continue turning the oxygen knob in the same direction to generate an even flame.

4 To turn off the torch, always shut down the oxygen first, and then turn off the gas.

LEFT: **Christel van der Laan**
Wave Series, 1998. Round, each 4.8 cm in diameter; square, 6 x 6 cm. 24-karat gold, 22-karat gold, sterling silver, copper, rusted mild steel, opal; hand fabricated, die formed, roller printed, corrugated, granulation, inlaid. Photo © Victor France

RIGHT: **Estelle Renée Vernon**
Japanese Textile Series: Grasses Brooch with Triangular Keum Boo, 2003. 5 x 2.3 x 0.6 cm. Sterling silver, 24-karat gold; kum boo, hand fabricated, etched, die formed. Photo © Robert Diamante

FAR RIGHT: **Jennifer Hall**
Winter Twig, 2002. 11.4 x 14 x 2.5 cm. Sterling silver; cast, hand fabricated, fine silver finished, oxidized. Photo © Doug Yaple

Lighting a Basic Acetylene B Tank with Ambient Oxygen

1 Slightly turn the knob on the hand piece counterclockwise (to the left), approximately one-eighth of a turn. You should not hear the gas escaping while you are lighting the torch.

2 Ignite the gas coming from the tip of the torch with a striker.

3 Adjust the size of the flame based on your soldering needs. (Practice heating various objects with different size flames to determine the flame you need.)

4 To turn off the torch, simply turn the knob on the hand piece clockwise (to the right).

BENCH TIP

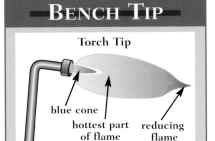

Torch Tip

blue cone

hottest part of flame

reducing flame

To vary the amount of heat from your torch, alter the size of the flame. If you have a mini-torch hand piece, you can switch tips for different size flames and amounts of localized heat.

Annealing

Annealing is the process by which hard metal is heated to make it softer and easier to work. Heat causes the molecules in the metal to stretch out after they have been compressed through work hardening. Each metal has a specific temperature at which it anneals. Some metals must be quenched immediately after heating, while others need to air cool.

Annealing Copper & Sterling Silver Sheet

MATERIALS
Copper or sterling silver sheet

TOOLS & SUPPLIES
Soldering kit, page 27

STEP BY STEP

1 Place the copper or sterling silver sheet to be annealed on the soldering block.

2 Light the torch and adjust the flame so that it is bushy and hot.

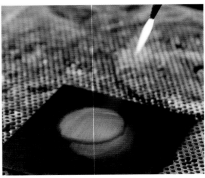

3 Heat the metal with the flame until the whole piece is almost red hot. (Look for a whitish color to appear underneath the flame.)

4 Using the copper tongs to handle the annealed metal, immediately quench it in water.

BENCH TIP

Thick pieces of metal may have to be annealed several times in order to anneal the piece completely.

Annealing Thin Wire

Thick wire can be annealed in the same manner as sheet metal, but to anneal a long section of thin wire, follow this process.

MATERIALS
Thin copper or sterling silver wire

TOOLS & SUPPLIES
Soldering kit, page 27

STEP BY STEP

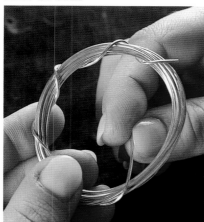

1 Wind the wire into a tight coil that is approximately 3 inches (7.6 cm) in diameter. Make sure no stray wire sticks out of the coil. Tightly wrap the ends of the wire around the coil to hold it in place.

2 Light the torch and adjust the flame so it is gentle and bushy. Slowly heat the coil as if it were one piece of solid metal, being sure not to heat one section more than another, until it is almost red hot.

3 Using the copper tongs to handle the annealed wire, immediately drop the coil into the water to quench it.

BENCH TIPS

Do not hold the annealed wire coil with tongs while quenching. The tongs will prevent part of the coil from quenching as quickly as the rest of the coil, and the tong-covered section will not be as fully annealed.

Drop the wire into the water with care, because some water might splash up.

Raising a Fine Silver Surface

This process brings a layer of fine silver to the surface of a sheet of sterling silver, preparing it for use with certain techniques, such as kum boo, enameling, and granulation.

MATERIALS
Sterling silver sheet

TOOLS & SUPPLIES
Soldering kit, page 27
Brass brush
Liquid soap

STEP BY STEP

1 Use a torch to heat the sterling silver sheet gently until its copper oxides come to the surface. Pickle the metal.

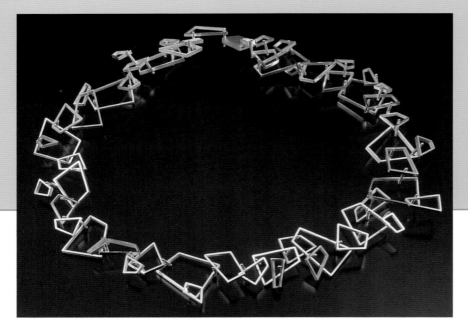

LEFT: **Dallae Kang**
Quadrangle Necklace, 2000. 2.5 x 25 x 25 cm.
14-karat gold, sterling silver; hand fabricated.
Photo © Helen Shirk

RIGHT: **Dallae Kang**
For Audrey Hepburn, 2001. 6.5 x 15.3 x 16.5
cm. Sterling silver, cubic zirconias, magnet; hand
fabricated, hinged. Photo © Helen Shirk

FAR RIGHT: **Charles Lewton-Brain**
Pin, Inlay, Painted Sheet, 1997. 7 x 4.5 x 1 cm.
Copper, sterling silver, 24-karat gold, patina; fusion
inlay, plated, scored, soldered, bent. Photo © artist

2 Use a brass brush, liquid soap, and water to clean the metal, and then dry it.

3 Repeat steps 1 through 3 until the surface of the sterling silver remains frosty white when heated.

Soldering

Soldering is a technique using heat to join metal, and solder is, in essence, a heat-activated metal "glue." There are numerous soldering methods. At times, you may have several options for producing the desired joint. Under other circumstances, a specific soldering procedure must be followed strictly for a successful result.

There are three prerequisites for soldering: the metal to be joined must be clean; the surfaces to be soldered must be touching; and flux must be applied to the joint. Clean metal means that the surface is free of dirt, grease, wax, and oxidation. If the metal that you order from the mill has not been left out to oxidize over a long period of time, it is often in good condition for soldering.

Selecting Solders

It is best to begin soldering with a high-temperature solder, and perform subsequent soldering operations with lower-temperature solders, no matter which metals

are being joined. There are several methods for using solder, and three are described in the directions that follow. Alternative ways to solder for particular techniques will be discussed later in the book.

Stick Soldering

Stick soldering is a method in which wire-form solder is applied by holding a length of it in your fingers or with tweezers. This application is most useful for soldering larger joints, such as hollow forms, or longer joints, such as a bezel to a back plate.

MATERIALS
Metal to be joined
Wire solder

TOOLS & SUPPLIES
Soldering kit, page 27

STEP BY STEP

1 Clean the metal pieces and position them on the soldering block so they are touching where they are to be joined. Apply flux to the metal.

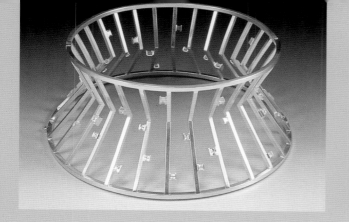

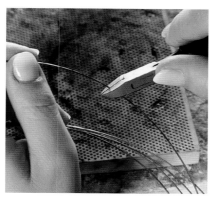

2 Cut a length of wire solder approximately 6 to 7 inches (15.2 to 17.8 cm) long. (You can hold long lengths of solder in your hand, but as it shortens with use, hold it in cross-locking tweezers to prevent burns.)

3 Light the torch and adjust the flame. Begin heating the metal slowly so the flux doesn't bubble up too quickly and make the metal move. Aim most of the heat on the area to be soldered, but also heat the surrounding areas so the rest of the metal doesn't act as a heat sink.

4 Once the heated flux looks glassy, test the temperature of the metal by gently touching the end of the solder stick to the metal you want to solder. If the metal is hot enough, the solder will immediately begin to flow. If the solder does not flow immediately, remove the solder stick and continue heating the metal. Retest the metal with the solder stick until the solder flows. Once the solder flows, remove the heat. Pickle and rinse the soldered metal.

BENCH TIPS

Aim the heat on the metal to be soldered, not on the solder stick. If it gets too hot, the solder stick will melt before it is put on the metal.

When introducing the solder stick, you may need to remove the flame from the metal quickly, and then quickly bring the flame back once the stick is in position.

Snippet Soldering

Snippet soldering, also called paillon soldering, is useful for applications requiring a minimum amount of solder, such as soldering jump rings closed.

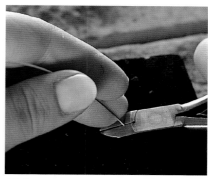

Making Snippets

Turn the snips so the cutting jaws are facing up, and place the snips on a hard surface, such as a spare soldering block. Use the snips to cut very small pieces of solder from a length of wire solder. As shown in the photo, snip the solder pieces so they are trapped underneath the jaws of the snips. (This method prevents the snippets from flying when you cut them.) Keep the snippets on a heat-resistant surface.

BENCH TIP

You can cut snippets to different lengths for different uses.

MATERIALS
Metal to be joined
Wire solder

TOOLS & SUPPLIES
Soldering kit, page 27

STEP BY STEP

1 Clean the metal to be soldered and position it on the soldering block. Apply flux to the area to be soldered (photo A). Apply a small amount of flux to the end of the solder pick so it is sticky with flux when heated (photo B).

BENCH TIP

Use the solder pick to hold the snippet in the right spot as needed, but use a light touch so the metal you are soldering doesn't move.

2 Light the torch and adjust the flame. With the solder pick in one hand and the torch in the other, simultaneously use the heat of the flame to melt the flux on the solder pick and pick up a snippet with the solder pick. (The heat of the torch must be in the same vicinity as the snippet and the solder pick or the snippet will not stick to the pick.)

3 Simultaneously move the torch flame and the solder pick with the snippet to the joint to be soldered.

4 Heat the metal with the flame, and then place the snippet on the joint. Let the solder flow and remove the heat.

5 The snippet can sit on the joint if the metal is not yet hot enough for the solder to flow. Once the metal is hot enough, the snippet should simply flow into the joint. Pickle and rinse the soldered metal.

Pick-up Soldering

In pick-up soldering, a snippet is melted directly onto the end of the smaller metal piece that is being soldered. The snippet is then remelted to join the small piece to the larger metal piece. This method is useful for tasks such as attaching an ear post to an earring. It decreases work time because one of the pieces being soldered is used to transport the solder.

MATERIALS

Metal to be joined, 1 large piece and 1 small piece
Wire solder

TOOLS & SUPPLIES

Soldering kit, page 27

STEP BY STEP

2 Pick up the small metal piece with the cross-locking tweezers, and dip the end to be soldered into the flux.

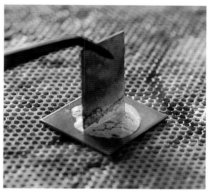

4 Use the torch to heat the large metal piece on the soldering block. When it is hot enough that the flux looks glassy, place the small piece with the solder into position on the larger piece. Continue heating the metal with the torch until the solder reflows (see photo). Remove the heat from the piece. Pickle and rinse the soldered metal.

1 Clean the metal to be joined and place the larger piece on the soldering block. Apply flux to the area to be soldered.

3 Light the torch and adjust the flame. Gently heat the end of the small metal piece. Melt a solder snippet onto the small piece in the location to be soldered.

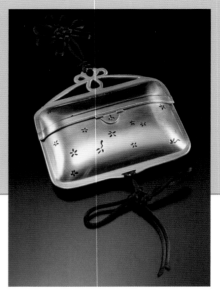

Pickling

A

To pickle metal after soldering, simply let the piece air cool slightly, and then place it in the pickle until it's clean. Using copper tongs, remove the metal from the pickle (photo A), and rinse it under cold water or in a solution of water and baking soda to neutralize any acid that may remain.

B

C

When pickle is spent it does not clean metal as quickly as it should and looks quite green in color. At this point, carry the pot to the sink, add a fair amount of baking soda to neutralize the acid (photo B), run water over the bubbling mixture (photo C), and then wash the neutralized acid down the sink.

Firescale

Firescale, an oxide of copper that occurs within sterling silver and some gold alloys, is one of the most persistent problems in metal-smithing. In practical terms, when these metals are heated, a reddish purple stain appears on their surface. To prevent firescale, you can coat an entire metal piece in a solution of boric acid and alcohol, burn off the alcohol with a torch, apply flux, and then solder as usual. The longer a piece is heated, the more chance it has of developing firescale. After multiple soldering operations, you'll have to contend with it. To remove firescale, you have to sand it off. This can be somewhat laborious, but it must be done in order to make good jewelry.

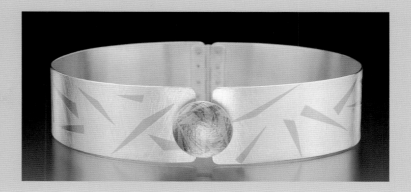

Finishing

The finish of a piece of jewelry enhances and completes its design, so finishing skills are an integral component of metalwork. There are many finishing options. A piece can be shiny or matte or have a *patina*, a coloration or blackening of the metal.

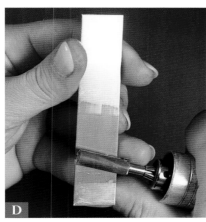

Sanding

The first step in preparing metal for finishing is to sand off any unwanted file marks or scratches. There are many options for sanding metal. Hand sanding is the most labor-intensive method and takes much longer than using a sanding attachment on a flexible shaft. Sanding discs, which snap directly onto a flexible shaft mandrel, are a quicker choice. Split mandrels are also available for the flexible shaft. A strip of sandpaper can be inserted into the slit and wrapped around the split mandrel (photo D). Plastic bristle discs and mizzy wheels can also be used for sanding. Experiment with these choices to find the ones that work best for you.

When using abrasive papers, I usually start with 220-grit sandpaper to remove most scribe lines and deeper marks. Next, I use 400-grit paper and completely sand over the first pass. A good practice is to sand with the 220-grit paper in one direction, and then sand over the same area with the 400-grit paper in the opposite direction. This way you'll know when the piece has been thoroughly sanded with the finer grit. Some jewelers suggest sanding with 600-grit paper before completely finishing, but I find this to be an unnecessary step unless I want an extremely high polish on the piece. Experiment both ways to discover your preference.

Matte Finishing

Use 400-grit sandpaper, steel wool of various grits, or a green kitchen scrub pad to create a matte finish by hand. Simply rub one of these abrasives back and forth or in a circular motion on a metal surface. A tumbler also creates a uniform matte finish, and there are many products that can be added to a tumbler to produce this effect. I use a ceramic cone media and some deburring compound. Place the metal in the tumbler with ceramic media, water, and deburring compound and let the tumbler run overnight. Experiment with other media and vary the tumbling time to see the range of matte finishes that can be achieved.

From left: tumbler, ceramic cone media, deburring compound

Polishing

To create a shiny finish with hand tools, use steel brush attachments in the flexible shaft, a soft-bristled brass brush, or a polishing cloth. Heavy-grit steel wool will also create a somewhat shiny finish. A shiny finish can also be gained by using stainless steel shot in a tumbler or by using a polishing machine. To use the steel shot, place approximately 2 pounds (0.9 kg) of mixed shot into the tumbler. (This amount is for a ½-gallon [1.9 L] tumbler. Adjust the amount of shot as needed.) Add to the tumbler enough water to cover the shot and a drop or two of dishwashing soap. The soap helps the steel burnish the metal gently. The steel shot shines the metal by continuously bombarding it with different shapes and burnishing it with each touch. Always use stainless steel shot so rust will not form in the tumbler. After several hours, the thoroughly beat and burnished metal has a shiny appearance.

Using a Polishing Machine

A mirror finish, the shiniest of all, can be achieved with a polishing machine and the right compounds and wheels. Three levels of polishing compounds, known as *tripoli*, *bobbing compound*, and *rouge*, are required. Three cotton buffing wheels will also be needed, one dedicated to each compound. It is wise to have a buffing wheel not only for each compound but also for each type of metal being polished. It is especially important to have separate wheels for steel items, because the steel from the wheel can become embedded in softer metals.

Clockwise from top: polishing wheels, tripoli polishing compound, rouge polishing compound, ring polishing wheel, bobbing compound

Clockwise from top: tumbler, steel shot, polishing cloth, heavy-grit steel wool, steel brush attachments for flexible shaft, brass brush

Polishing machine

MATERIALS
Tripoli, bobbing, and rouge
  polishing compounds
Metal to be polished
Dishwashing liquid

TOOLS & SUPPLIES
Polishing machine
3 cotton buffing wheels
Soft-bristle toothbrush
Ultrasonic cleaner (optional)

STEP BY STEP

1 Turn on the polishing machine and gently place the hole of the tripoli-compound cotton buffing wheel on the rotating spindle (see photo). Let go of the wheel, and the centrifugal force of the rapidly turning spindle will pull the wheel into place.

2 Run the block of tripoli polishing compound against the buffing wheel.

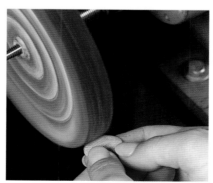

3 Hold the metal to be polished firmly in both hands, about halfway down from the center of the buffing wheel. Gently rub the metal on the wheel and move it around slowly and firmly to ensure an even polish. Because the polishing compound actually removes metal, don't hold the piece in one place for very long or ruts will form on the surface.

4 Repeat steps 1–3 with the bobbing compound and the rouge, changing buffing wheels on the polishing machine for each compound.

5 Remove any polishing compound residue left on the metal by gently scrubbing it with a soft-bristle toothbrush and some degreasing dishwashing liquid, or let the piece soak in an ultrasonic cleaner.

Patinas

There are many patinas you can apply to a metal surface. Silver, copper, brass, and nickel silver take a patina quite easily, while gold, platinum, titanium, and niobium do not. The disparity in how different metals accept a patina can be used creatively, such as blackening a silver component in a mixed-metal piece while leaving the gold element its natural color. The most common agents used to blacken metal are liver of sulfur and selenium toner, a chemical agent used in photography.

Liver of Sulfur

Silver, brass, and copper can be blackened in a liver of sulfur solution. This simple patina adds color and depth to jewelry and makes surface designs and textures more visible. Liver of sulfur has a strong odor, so use it outside or in a well-ventilated area.

MATERIALS
Liver of sulfur
Hot water
Metal to be blackened

TOOLS & SUPPLIES
Glass bowl
Rubber gloves
Copper tongs
Steel wool, abrasive cleanser, or green scrub pad (optional)

STEP BY STEP

1 In a glass bowl, dissolve one chunk of liver of sulfur in hot water.

2 While wearing protective rubber gloves, drop the metal to be blackened into the liver-of-sulfur solution (see photo). Leave the metal in the solution until it turns black, approximately 1 to 2 minutes. (If you leave the piece in the solution too long, the black patina becomes a thick crust that can flake off.)

3 Use copper tongs to remove the metal from the liver of sulfur (see photo). Wash the metal in hot water to help adhere the patina. Repeat steps 2 and 3 if a blacker tone is desired.

4 Leave the piece black or rub it with an abrasive material, such as steel wool, an abrasive cleanser, or a green scrub pad. This rubbing gives the metal a finish that lets the natural color of the metal come through the patina.

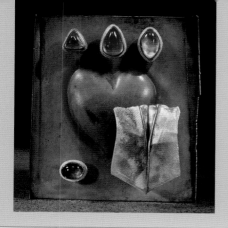

Selenium Toner

Selenium toner quickly and easily creates a black patina on silver, brass, and copper. Like all chemicals, selenium toner must be used in a well-ventilated area. Wear rubber gloves to protect your hands.

MATERIALS
Selenium toner
Metal to be blackened
Warm water

TOOLS & SUPPLIES
Rubber gloves
Glass bowl
Copper tongs or piece of non-steel wire
Steel wool, abrasive cleanser, or green scrub pad (optional)

STEP BY STEP

1 Wearing rubber gloves, pour the selenium toner into a glass bowl. Place the metal to be blackened into the solution and wait approximately 15 seconds.

2 Use copper tongs or a piece of non-steel wire to remove the metal from the solution. Wash the metal in warm water. Repeat this process to darken the patina, if desired.

Oxidation

Intentional heat oxidation causes some metals to change color. Copper accepts this patina especially well.

MATERIALS
Metal to be oxidized
Wax or clear lacquer

TOOLS & SUPPLIES
Soldering block
Soldering torch

STEP BY STEP

1 Place the metal to be oxidized on the soldering block. Light the torch and adjust the flame.

2 Run the torch flame over the metal until its surface color changes. Once the color changes, stop heating the metal immediately and let it air cool.

3 Seal the oxidation with wax or a clear lacquer.

Metal Coloring

There are many innovative methods for adding color to metal jewelry. Drawing directly on the metal with colored pencils, markers, or paints provides an infinite color palette and can create some amazing details and finishes. Use a clear acrylic spray finish or lacquer to preserve this type of coloration.

Reversible Pendant

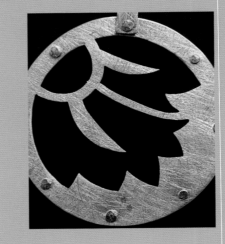

Sterling silver sheets are pierced with different motifs, and then positioned on either side of opaque acrylic. Wire rivets secure the layers and complete the modern design.

MATERIALS

Sterling silver sheet, 24 gauge
Photocopied design templates,
    page 172
Black acrylic sheet (or color of your
    choice), 1/8 inch (3 mm) thick
Sterling silver round wire, 18 gauge
Commercial neck wire with clasp

TOOLS & SUPPLIES

Bench tool kit, page 27

STEP BY STEP

1 Use separators to draw two 1 1/2-inch (3.8 cm) circles onto the 24-gauge sterling silver sheet. Use the jeweler's saw to cut out the circles, and then file the cut edges smooth.

2 Transfer one photocopied design template onto each circle. Pierce and saw out the transferred designs.

3 Use the jeweler's saw to cut a circle out of the 1/8-inch-thick (3 mm) acrylic. Make the circle slightly larger than 1 1/2 inches (3.8 cm) in diameter.

4 Give the front side of each pierced silver circle the final finish you desire. (I used 400-grit sandpaper to create a matte finish on my circles.)

5 Use a 1-mm bit in the flexible shaft to drill holes on each of the silver discs. Drill the holes at the 3 o'clock and 9 o'clock positions, as indicated on the design templates.

6 Line up one drilled silver disc with the acrylic circle, and drill the holes through the acrylic.

7 Using the 18-gauge sterling silver wire, rivet through the drilled holes to attach the three pendant layers.

8 Continue to drill and rivet the remaining holes as indicated on the design template, but do not rivet the top hole for the bale—just drill it.

9 Use the jeweler's saw or bastard file to remove all excess acrylic sheet from around the silver discs. Make the three pendant layers even on the edges.

10 Use the jeweler's saw to cut a rectangle out of the 24-gauge silver sheet that is 3 x 20 mm. Sand the edges of the cut metal.

11 Use the flexible shaft to drill a 1-mm hole in each end of the silver rectangle. Center the holes on the width of the rectangle and make them approximately 2 mm from each end.

12 Determine the center of the silver rectangle and bend it at this point to make an even U shape for the bale.

13 Rivet the bale to the top hole of the pendant.

14 Sand both sides of each rivet to remove any burrs.

15 Thread the pendant on the commercial neck wire.

Chased Barrette

Use basic metalworking skills to create a hair accessory that is incredibly attractive and functional. Chase a simple pattern onto a nickel silver disc, rivet it to a commercial clasp, and you've got a one-of-a-kind barrette.

MATERIALS

Nickel silver sheet, 24 gauge
Commercial barrette clasp
Silver tubing, 3 to 4 mm in outside
    diameter (OD)

TOOLS & SUPPLIES

Bench tool kit, page 27

STEP BY STEP

1 Use separators to draw a 3-inch (7.6 cm) circle onto the nickel silver sheet.

2 Use the jeweler's saw to cut out the circle. File the edges smooth, and then sand them to a 400-grit finish.

3 Use the chasing or stamping tools of your choice to chase a design onto the metal circle.

4 Place the chased metal circle upside down in a low depression on a dapping block. Use a wooden dap to dome the metal slightly.

5 Place the commercial barrette clasp on the inside of the domed metal circle. Use a pencil or scribe to mark the holes in the clasp onto the domed metal. These are the points where the clasp will be riveted to the circle.

6 Use the flexible shaft and a bit that is the same size as the silver tubing to drill the holes marked in step 5.

7 Use the jeweler's saw to cut the silver tubing to the appropriate length for riveting the clasp to the domed metal circle. Sand the cut tubing ends.

8 Position the barrette clasp on the domed metal circle. Rivet one side of the clasp to the circle, and then the other. (If the barrette clasp is too long for the circle, saw off the excess length at the ends, but be sure to leave the rivet holes intact.)

9 Patina the barrette, and then rub its surface with a green kitchen scrub or steel wool. This allows the patina to remain in the chasing while giving the metal surface a smooth shine.

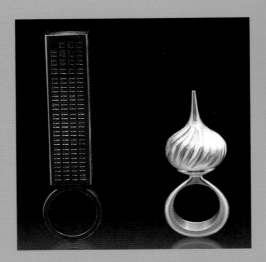

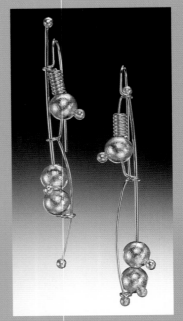

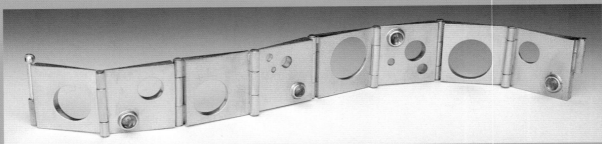

TOP LEFT: Natalya Pinchuk
Building Ring and Dome Ring, 2003 and 2001. Left, 8 x 2.5 x 2.5 cm. Sterling silver, 22-karat gold, patina, colored marker; hand fabricated, plated, etched, oxidized, smithed, cast, chased. Photo © artist

TOP RIGHT: Debra Lynn Gold
Tango Earrings, 2004. Each, 7 x 1 x 1 cm. Sterling silver; formed, hand fabricated, file finished. Photo © Ralph Gabriner

CENTER: K.C. Calum
Untitled, 2004. 17 x 2.8 x 0.8 cm. Sterling silver, amethyst; cast, fabricated. Photo © artist

BOTTOM LEFT & RIGHT: Masumi Kataoka
Telling Time with One's Fragments #1 and #2, 2002. Each, 4 x 10 x 7 cm. Sterling silver, 14-karat gold, 24-karat gold, plated. Photos © Ingrid Psuty (main) and artist (detail)

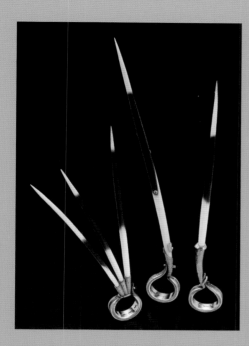

TOP LEFT: **Andy Cooperman**
3 Quill Rings, 2004. Tallest, 22.9 cm. Sterling silver, gold, porcupine quills; fabricated, riveted, oxidized. Photo © Doug Yaple

TOP RIGHT: **Natasha Wozniak**
Scrolling Flourish Bracelet, 2004. 6.5 x 3 cm. Sterling silver, iolite; forged, bent, soldered. Photo © Ralph Gabriner

BOTTOM LEFT: **Chris Irick**
Oval Brooch Series II, 2004. Each, 6 x 3 x 1.5 cm. Sterling silver, fine silver, acrylic; fabricated, carved, die formed, pierced. Photo © artist

BOTTOM RIGHT: **Roberta** and **David Williamson**
My Garden, 1998. Average size, 13 x 4 x 1 cm. Sterling silver, patina; hand fabricated, chased, textured, formed. Photo © James Beards

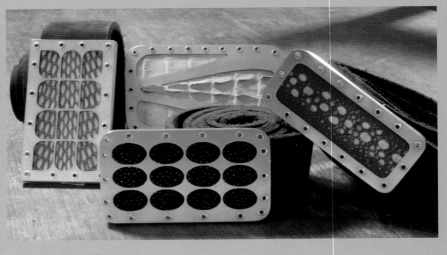

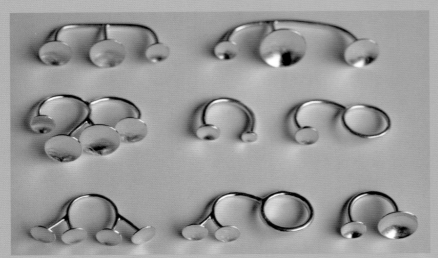

TOP LEFT: Joanna Gollberg
Money Leaf Brooch, 2000. 7.6 x 7 x 0.3 cm. Sterling silver, nickel silver; marriage of metal, fabricated. Photo © Seth Tice-Lewis

TOP RIGHT: Ruth Avra
Untitled, 2005. Largest, 6.4 x 8.9 cm. Sterling silver, copper, cobra, stingray, caiman stingray, nubuck leather; sawed, soldered, riveted. Photo © Tania Quintanilla tqphoto.com

CENTER LEFT: Judith Renstrom
Untitled, 2004. 8.5 x 7.5 x 1 cm. 14-karat gold, sterling silver, faceted moonstones; folded, matrix die formed, hand fabricated, oxidized. Photo © Hub Willson

CENTER RIGHT: Joanna Gollberg
Three Brooches, 2004. Largest, 3.8 x 2.5 x 0.6 cm. Sterling silver, 18-karat gold, sapphires, diamonds, garnets; hollow formed, fabricated, flush set. Photo © Steve Mann

BOTTOM LEFT: Colleen Baran
Floating Saucer Series Rings, 2002–2005. From 2.5 x 6.4 x 2.5 to 2 x 2.3 x 0.9 cm. Sterling silver; hand fabricated, dapped. Photo © artist

Forming Metal

To form metal is to alter its shape. The simplest way of doing this is with your own hands, but there are many more options available, including forging with a hammer, dapping in a block, die forming with a hydraulic press, and creating repoussé in pitch. At the end of this chapter, on pages 80–83, you will find two projects that use scoring and bending and dapping to form metal.

Bending & Shaping

Bending Sheet Metal

To make a straight bend in sheet metal, begin by bending the metal with your fingers. Once an angle is started, place it on the edge of a steel block and use a wooden or rawhide mallet to hammer a sharp edge as shown in photo A. To create an edge that is more crisp and stiff, use the flat face of metal hammer, such as a chasing hammer, along the bend (photo B).

As shown in photo C, you can also use a vise to bend sheet metal in a straight line.

All types of pliers can be used to bend small sections of sheet metal. Round-nose pliers are useful for curving small areas, and flat-nose pliers are good for making small bends.

Bending Wire

Wire can be manipulated into all sorts of designs. Your fingers are good tools for bending wire because they are strong and don't leave any imprints on the metal. Use a pair of hand pliers to form tighter, more precise bends, or use pliers to hold the wire steady while you bend the wire with your fingers. Wire can also be bent around mandrels of different shapes, such as round, square, and oval mandrels.

Making a Wire Jig

A wire jig is handy for bending wire into uniform shapes. Commercial wire jigs are available, but you can also make your own.

MATERIALS
Block of wood large enough to accommodate wire design
Thin finish nails, 1 to 1½ inches (2.5 to 3.8 cm) long
Wire of your choice

TOOLS & SUPPLIES
Bench tool kit, page 27

STEP BY STEP

1 Create the wire design and draw it on the block of wood.

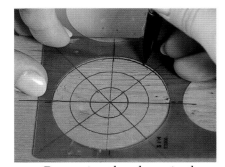

2 Determine the places in the design where the wire curves or bends, and mark these places on the wooden block. For a sharp bend, make only one mark. For a gentle curve, make a line of dots. A nail will be hammered into the block at each marked spot, so leave enough room between dots to accommodate their thickness.

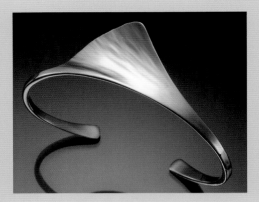

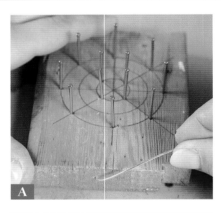

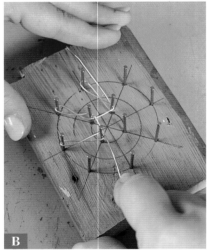

3 Using a bit that is approximately one-half the diameter
of the finishing nails, drill a hole
at each mark. These pilot holes
help prevent the nails from split-
ting the wood as they are hammered into the block.

4 Use the hammer to drive one
finishing nail into each
predrilled hole. Leave from ½ to
1 inch (1.3 to 2.5 cm) of each nail
sticking out of the wood.

5 Drill a hole in the wood block
where you will start the wire
design. Prior to bending the wire
around the jig, make a 90-degree
bend in one wire end. Place this
bend in the hole (photo A) so the
wire will stay firmly in place as you
bend it around the nails (photo B).
This step produces some metal
waste, but it can help create accurate wire shapes.

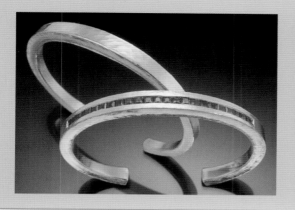

Forging

Forging alters the thickness and shape of metal through the force of a hammer. By applying this force from different directions, the metal can be stretched or condensed. It is necessary to have a sturdy metal support surface underneath the metal being forged, such as a stake or an anvil, and the proper hammer for specific forging processes.

The most basic forging techniques are tapering the length of a square or round wire and widening a piece of stock metal. Both ways of moving metal are performed in a calculated and controlled manner.

MATERIALS
Copper, silver, or gold bar stock, square or round, size dependent on project*

TOOLS & SUPPLIES
Chair with adjustable height
Anvil
Tree stump or other anvil support
Hearing protection
Forging hammer
Soldering kit, page 27
Planishing hammer
File (optional)
220- and 400-grit sandpaper (optional)

I recommend practicing forging on a piece of copper bar stock that is 5 or 10 mm thick.

STEP BY STEP

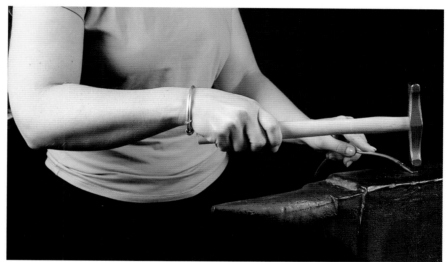

1 Adjust your chair to the proper height in relation to the height of the anvil on the tree stump. Your forearm, wrist, and hammer should all be in alignment, with room left for making hammer blows (see photo). If this position does not feel relaxed and you begin to ache after hammering, readjust the chair.

2 Put on the hearing protection. Hold the forging hammer so it will move loosely within your grip and your hand will feel relatively stress-free. If you are using unnecessary force, your wrist and arm will begin to ache, so ease up and make yourself relax.

3 Begin making hammer blows at the place where you want the metal to stretch, letting the weight of the hammer do all the work (photo C). Make your hammer blows count. The metal will move with each blow, so precision is desirable. To taper the metal, position the face of the hammer

BENCH TIPS

When tapering a round bar, it is helpful first to stretch the metal and form it into a square (see photo). Then, go back and hammer the square corners until the edges are curved and the bar returns to its round shape.

If a square bar becomes rectangular while being tapered and you want it to remain square, turn the bar 90 degrees and continue hammering to re-square the metal.

If you have widened the metal in a curved fashion, you may need to clean up the curve with a file. Experiment to see what results you achieve when you hammer directly on the thin edge of the curve. You can thicken the edge of a forged piece by lightly hammering directly onto the edge at a 90-degree angle.

perpendicular to the length of the bar (photo B). To widen the metal, the face of the hammer should be parallel to the length of the bar (photo C).

4 As soon as the hammer blows make a pinging sound instead of a dull thud, anneal the metal (see page 48). Thoroughly dry the metal after annealing to prevent the anvil and hammer from rusting.

5 Once the metal is close to being sufficiently tapered or widened, planish the metal. (Planishing means removing any forging marks with the slightly curved side of the planishing hammer until the metal surface is as smooth as it can be.) Planishing does stretch the metal a bit, so take this into account when determining when to stop forging.

6 If you wish to clean the forged stock completely, file off any facets (bumps made from the planishing hammer), and then sand the piece with 220- and 400-grit sandpaper.

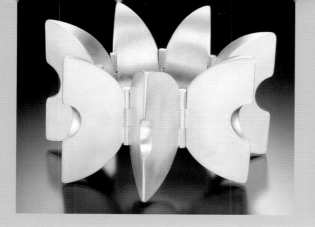

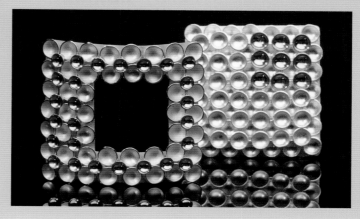

Dapping

Dapping sheet metal produces dome shapes that are functional in many areas of jewelry fabrication.

MATERIALS
Sheet metal of your choice

TOOLS & SUPPLIES
Bench tool kit, page 27

STEP BY STEP

1 Saw out the shape to be domed from the sheet metal.

2 Select the depression in the dapping block that has the appropriate depth and curvature for the dome you want to create. Place the sheet metal shape in the selected depression. If the metal is too large for the depression, choose another depression close to the desired dome size in which the metal fits.

3 Choose a dapping punch that closely fits the size of the selected depression. Use a mallet to hammer the punch gently into the depression, forcing the metal down (see photo). To ensure that the metal stretches evenly and its surface is evenly domed, aim the punch at the edges of the metal first, and then carefully move the punch into the center of the metal. In many cases an uneven stretch is inconsequential, but in some situations, such as when stones are set in the domed metal, uniform thickness is important.

4 To form a dome with a tighter curve, move the metal to the next smaller depression in the block, select the proper punch, and continue dapping. Repeat this step until you achieve the desired dome.

Dapping a Half-Sphere

Dapping a perfect half-sphere is tricky. You must use punches that are smaller than the size of the depression. Dap the dome with the smaller dapping punch until it seems as if the dome might form around the head of the punch, then move the metal to a smaller depression and use a smaller punch until a half sphere is achieved. To determine whether a true half sphere has been created, measure the dome with calipers. Its height should be exactly half of its width.

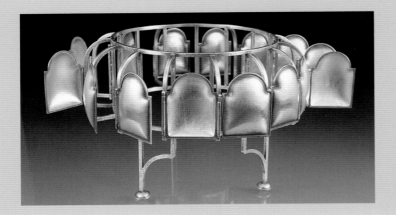

Die Forming

You can create an infinite number of three-dimensional metal forms and shapes through die forming. This technique uses a hydraulic press to push metal into a prescribed shape.

New Tool *A hydraulic press is a machine that exerts a large force to press metal into dies or into unusual shapes. A typical hydraulic press can exert up to 20 tons (18.1 metric tons) of pressure on an object, making it an excellent choice for stretching metal in its cold, hard state.*

MATERIALS

Die, $1/4$ inch (0.6 cm) steel or $3/8$ to $1/2$ inch (1 to 1.3 cm) acrylic*
Nonferrous sheet metal, 20 to 26-gauge
Steel sheet, if needed

TOOLS & SUPPLIES

Bench tool kit, page 27
Soldering kit, page 27
Tape (optional)
Tough rubber, approximately $1/4$ to $1/2$ inch (0.6 to 1.3 cm) thick
20-ton (18.1 metric ton) hydraulic press (minimum pressure)

Most jewelry-making dies are no larger than 4 x 4 inches (10.2 x 10.2 cm) for ease of use and to fit the hydraulic press. If you are making an extremely deep form, I recommend using the thicker-gauge metal. If the metal will have a fairly low dome, use the thinner-gauge metal.

Clockwise from top center: carved steel block die, acrylic sheet, rubber sheets, acrylic dies

STEP BY STEP
Making the Die

1 Create a design and scribe it onto the die. Leave a margin of approximately $1/2$ to 1 inch (1.3 to 2.5 cm) between the edge of the design and the edge of the die.

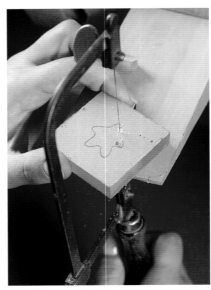

2 Using a bit large enough to accommodate the saw blade, drill a hole in the negative space to be cut out of the die. Saw out the negative shape, making sure you hold the saw frame at a 90-degree angle to the die (see photo).

3 File the cut edges of the design, and then sand the edges to a 220-grit finish. Make sure the top edge of the cutout shape is not sharp, especially if you are creating a steel die.

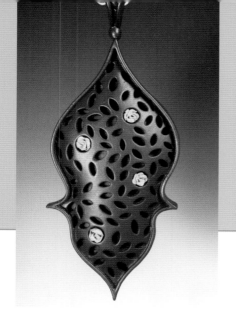

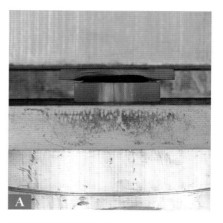

Forming the Metal

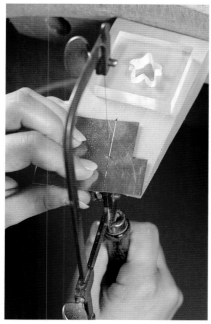

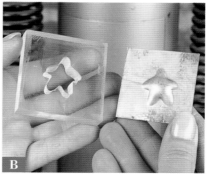

4 Using the jeweler's saw, cut the sheet metal into a square that is larger than the design but smaller than the die. (Extra metal is needed around the edges of the design because when the metal is pressed some of it is pulled into the cutout area to create the depth.) Anneal the sheet metal, and let it dry.

5 Position the sheet metal on the die. (You may want to tape the corners of the metal to the die, but because it can leave a sticky residue that must be cleaned off, I find this creates more trouble than it's worth.) Place the rubber on top of the sheet metal, and place the whole stack on the hydraulic press. (Depending on the press, you may need to place a small steel sheet on top of the rubber before placing the stack in the press.)

6 Turn on the hydraulic press and begin pressing the rubber into the die (photo A). As soon as you feel the action of the press firming up and becoming more difficult to move, release the pressure and check on the metal. If the depth of the design is insufficient, replace the stack in the press and continue pressing until the desired depth is achieved. Remove the formed metal from the die (photo B).

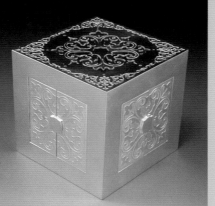

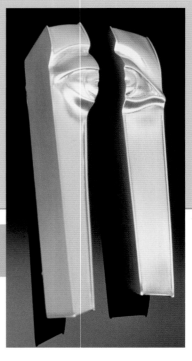

Some hydraulic presses have a pressure gauge, which can be extremely useful in determining the amount of pressure needed to make matching die forms. Record the pressure-gauge reading of a successful die form in a notebook for future reference.

If you hear a fairly loud pop when depressing the hydraulics, it may mean that too much pressure has been applied and the metal has stretched and literally popped open. If you don't have a pressure gauge, make an effort to remember the force it took to reach that stage, and avoid repeating it. Having a hydraulic press with no pressure gauge forces you to go through lots of trial and error, and you will most likely have many mistakes, so go slow in applying pressure in order to save material.

To achieve an especially deep form, take the metal out of the die during the forming process and reanneal it. This gives the metal more room to stretch without popping.

Experiment with different types of rubber. The rubber I like to use for die forming is a red variety originally intended for boat bumpers. Your local rubber dealer may sell scrap by the pound.

Scoring & Bending

There are many ways to bend sheet metal and wire into angles, but there is one way to make a sharp angle that is unsurpassed. This technique is called scoring and bending.

MATERIALS
Sheet metal or wire of your choice, any gauge

TOOLS & SUPPLIES
Bench tool kit, page 27
Soldering kit, page 27

STEP BY STEP

1 Use the saw to cut the sheet metal or wire to the desired dimensions. Determine the placement of the angle and use the scribe and stainless steel ruler to draw a line on the metal at this

location. Retrace the line with the scribe, deepening the line in the metal (see photo). This will be the guide line for filing, so the deeper it is scribed into the metal, the better.

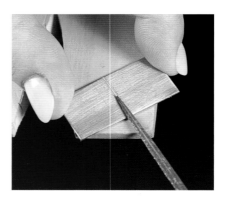

Figure 1

2 Hold the metal firmly on the bench pin. Using one 90-degree corner of the square file, begin slowly and strongly filing the scribed line (see photo). The goal is to file a 90-degree groove that very nearly penetrates the metal's surface (figure 1).

3 As you continue carefully filing the groove, frequently turn over the metal and check for the appearance of a thin line on the reverse side. This is a visual indicator to stop filing. If the metal is filed too much, it could break when it is bent.

4 Once you see the thin line on the reverse side, bend the metal into an angle. You may have only one chance to bend the metal into the proper angle. If you attempt to bend the metal back and forth, the thin surface remaining in the groove will work harden and the metal will snap into two pieces.

5 Hard solder the joint to secure the bent metal. Use a small snippet so the line remains clean.

Scoring with Separating Discs

When making hollow forms that require sharp angles, you can quickly cut a groove with a separating disc attachment on the flexible shaft. Because the separating disc is harder to control at times than a needle file, this is a riskier process. Safety goggles must be worn whenever you are using a separating disc. This attachment is notorious for breaking easily, and it can cause serious harm to your eyes.

To make a groove with a separating disc, carve a straight line down the metal where it is to be scored, and then gently use the separating disc to remove metal along both sides of the line to create an angled groove. Bend and solder the joint as usual. This alternate method is quite useful when making multiple sharp bends, especially when crisp, perfect angles are not the main goal.

Repoussé

In the ancient technique of repoussé, a raised decorative metal surface is created through the controlled stretching of sheet metal from its front and back sides. A repoussé surface can be freeform or precise, simple or extremely intricate. Repoussé is often used in conjunction with chasing, and it is most often seen on silver hollowware.

MATERIALS
Copper or silver sheet,
16 to 18 gauge

TOOLS & SUPPLIES
Bench tool kit, page 27
Soldering kit, page 27
Pitch
Olive oil (optional)
Liner tool

STEP BY STEP

1 Draw a repoussé pattern and determine how large to make the design. A good size for beginners is a 3 x 3-inch (7.6 x 7.6 cm) metal sheet. Use a saw to cut the metal to size, and then use a scribe to draw the design onto the metal.

2 Anneal the sheet metal, and dry it thoroughly.

3 Use the torch to warm the pitch gently and carefully without burning it. Keep a soft flame on the pitch and constantly move the flame around its surface. It takes a while to heat the pitch to the desired temperature. The surface should be soft like caramel candy, not

New Tool *When creating repoussé, jewelers use pitch, a thick, sticky substance, to give resistance to metal. Pitch can be obtained from coal tar, wood tar, or petroleum. These varieties are almost black in color and set up very stiffly. Pitch can also come from the sap of coniferous trees. This type sets up softer and is more malleable than darker pitch.*

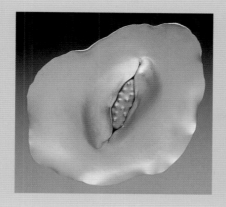

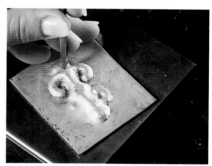

runny like molasses. The surface of the pitch can be coated with olive oil to keep the metal from sticking, but if this coating is applied too frequently, it can ruin the consistency of the pitch.

4 Let the top of the pitch cool down slightly, and then secure the metal into the pitch with the scribed design facing up. The pitch should rise some around the edge of the metal to secure it.

5 Begin punching the back side of the raised design into the

metal with dapping punches. The pitch gives some resistance, but it also gives room for the metal to stretch. (Dapping punches are useful for making domes in the metal. Use different punch sizes for different types of punching. To create other, more specific shapes, you may need to make custom repoussé tools.) Complete the back side of the design.

6 To work the front side, remove the metal from the pitch, turn it over, and place it on the steel block. Use punches and repoussé tools to push down any areas that need re-flattening and shape areas from the top of the sheet.

7 Continue punching and forming the metal, first on one side, and then on the other, both in the pitch and on the block (see photo). The metal will have to be annealed throughout the process of punching and forming. Near the end of the repoussé process, use a liner tool to further define the design.

8 Sand the finished piece carefully so the details of the repoussé and chasing remain intact. (You may need to have a preliminary sanding, and then go back and re-chase the piece.) Polish the metal or give it a matte finish (see pages 55–57).

BENCH TIP

To prevent fumes from burning pitch residue left on the metal, thoroughly clean the metal before each annealing.

Cuttlefish Casting

A cuttlefish is a squidlike mollusk that has ten arms and a calcareous internal shell. In this technique, the dried shell is used as a mold for casting. A cuttlefish mold can only be used once, though one fish can be cut into several pieces, depending on the size of the design. The most interesting characteristic of this technique is that the cuttlefish has growth lines visually similar to wood grain, thus creating a one-of-a-kind texture on the cast metal.

New Tool *A crucible is a vessel made of a material that does not easily melt. It is most frequently used in high-temperature applications, such as melting metal and supporting objects in the kiln.*

MATERIALS
    Dried cuttlefish
    Scrap metal of your choice
    Boric acid

TOOLS & SUPPLIES
    Bench tool kit, page 27
    Carving tools, such as a craft knife,
        burrs, a scribe, or a plastic knife
    Binding wire
    Ceramic crucible
    Soldering kit, page 27

Before You Begin
When it is time to heat and cast the metal (steps 7 through 9), have a partner on hand to hold the mold.

STEP BY STEP

1 Use the jeweler's saw to cut the cuttlefish into smaller pieces based on the size of your design. Hold the length of the cuttlefish parallel to the bench pin or cutting surface and saw through the width of the fish. (Most cuttlefish can be cut into two or three pieces.)

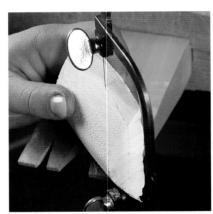

2 Use the jeweler's saw to cut one of the cuttlefish pieces made in step 1 in half, like a filet.

3 Rub the cut sides of the two halves together to create two flat surfaces with a perfect fit.

4 Use any of the carving tools to carve your design into one interior surface of the cuttlefish. The depth that is carved will be the thickness of the finished piece.

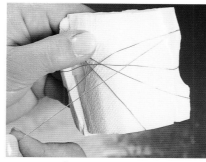

6 Put the two halves of the cuttlefish together and secure them with binding wire (see photo). Carve a larger indentation at the top of the cuttlefish where the sprue channel meets the top end.

8 While a studio partner or helper holds the cuttlefish with tongs, pour the red-hot metal into the sprue channel.

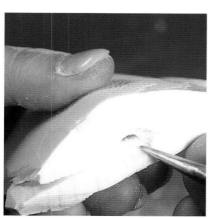

5 Carve a groove that is 3 to 5 mm in diameter from the design to the top end of the cuttlefish. This is the channel through which the molten metal is poured into the cuttlefish; it is known as a sprue channel.

7 Estimate the amount of scrap metal that will need to be melted. (It is better to overestimate the amount, because you can always stop pouring metal into the sprue channel.) Place the scrap metal in the ceramic crucible and add some boric acid. Heat the metal until it is red hot and completely molten.

9 Let the cuttlefish and the cast metal cool, and then open the mold (see photo). Finish the cast metal as desired.

Pyramid Earrings

The sharp lines created by scoring and bending inspired these dramatic earrings. This project introduces you to hollow-form construction and provides plenty of practice for soldering clean seams.

MATERIALS
   Sterling silver sheet, 22 gauge
   Sterling silver round wire, 20 gauge

TOOLS & SUPPLIES
   Bench tool kit, page 27
   Soldering kit, page 27

STEP BY STEP

1 Mark two rectangles on the 22-gauge sterling silver sheet, each 2.5 x 3.5 cm. Use the jeweler's saw to cut out these rectangles, and then file or sand their edges perfectly straight.

2 Measure and mark a line that is 1 cm inside the long edge of one metal rectangle. Measure and mark a second line that is 2 cm inside the long edge. Repeat this step on the second metal rectangle. Scribe the marked lines.

3 Following the directions for scoring on page 74, use one 90-degree corner of a square file to make a groove on the lines scribed in step 2.

4 One at a time, bend the scored metal rectangles to form a hollow triangle for each earring.

5 Using hard solder, solder both grooves in each earring for strength, and then solder the seam to close the hollow triangle. Pickle and rinse both triangles.

6 File both of the soldered triangles so all the corners are sharp.

7 Use the jeweler's saw to cut four small pieces of the 22-gauge sterling silver sheet. These will be used to cap the ends of the triangles, so make sure you cut them larger than the area that needs to be covered.

8 Flux the four sterling silver end caps, and then stick solder a dab of medium solder onto each end cap.

9 Flux the ends of the triangles. Place one end of each triangle on an end cap, and solder the seams. (The solder applied to the end caps in step 8 will remelt and secure the joint when heated.)

10 Turn the triangles over and solder on the remaining end caps to create a hollow form. Pickle and rinse the triangles.

11 Use the jeweler's saw to cut off any extra metal from the end caps. File all soldered end cap edges smooth, and then sand the edges to a 220-grit finish.

12 Cut two pieces of the 20-gauge sterling silver wire, each 2 inches (5.1 cm) long. Bend the end of each wire into an L shape, with the bottom section of the L being 8 to 10 mm long.

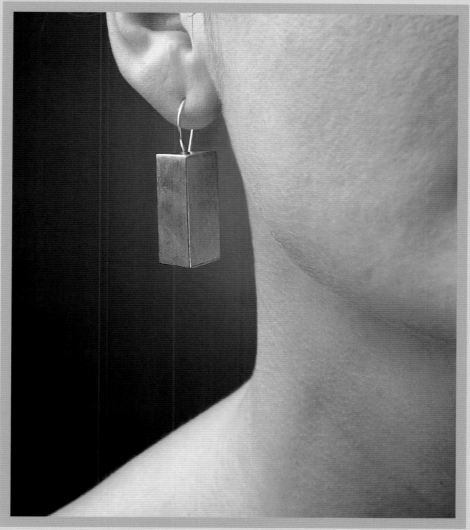

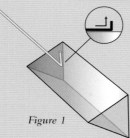

Figure 1

13 Using the pick-up solder method with easy solder, connect one L-shaped wire to the back of one earring as shown in figure 1. The smaller section of the L should be centered on the back of the hollow form and the longer section should extend from the top of the earring. Repeat this step on the second earring. Pickle and rinse the earrings.

14 On each earring, bend the longer section of wire (the ear wire) at a 90-degree angle toward the front of the earring, and then wrap the wire around a 10-mm mandrel toward the back of the earring.

15 For each earring, use round-nose pliers to bend the small section of the L-shaped wire into a hook to catch the ear wire.

16 Sand the ends of the ear wires and give the earrings a final finish. Rub the bent edges of the triangles with a burnisher to highlight the angles.

Bubble Brooch

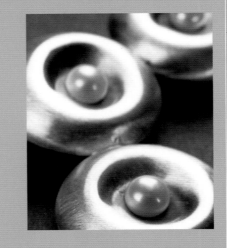

Sterling silver discs are domed, backed, dapped, and connected to create this playfully elegant brooch. Peg-set white pearls perfectly accentuate the rounded forms.

MATERIALS

8 sterling silver discs, 24 gauge, 1 inch (2.5 cm) in diameter
Sterling silver round wire, 22 gauge
Commercial pin catch, joint, and pin stem
4 round white pearls, half drilled, 5 mm

TOOLS & SUPPLIES

Bench tool kit, page 27
Soldering kit, page 27
Two-part epoxy resin
Wooden toothpicks

STEP BY STEP

1 Dap four of the sterling silver discs in a deep depression on the dapping block to create a fairly high dome in each disc.

2 Sand the bottom of each domed disc flat so the edges will make a solid solder joint with an undomed disc.

3 Use hard solder to solder each domed disc onto a flat disc, making a total of four hollow forms. Pickle and rinse the forms.

4 Use a jeweler's saw or file to remove any extra metal from around the edge of the hollow forms. File and sand the forms to a 400-grit finish.

5 Use a chasing hammer and a small dap (approximately 10 mm in diameter) to depress the middle of each form until the top of the domed metal touches the back sheet.

6 Place the metal forms on the soldering block and arrange them in an appealing configuration. Use the pick-up soldering method with medium solder to connect the forms. Equally heat each form so the solder joins them evenly. Pickle and rinse the metal.

7 Use the jeweler's saw to cut four 3- to 5-mm lengths of the 22-gauge round sterling silver wire.

8 Use the pick-up soldering method with easy solder to connect one short wire length to the center of each depression dapped in step 5. Pickle and rinse the metal.

9 Place the brooch on the soldering block with the flat side facing up. Arrange the commercial pin catch and joint on the back of the brooch so the pin stem fits between them well and its point does not protrude too far past the catch. Also, position the joint above the catch. (This layout helps prevent the brooch from falling off if the catch comes unfastened.) Solder the catch and the joint to the brooch with easy solder using the pick-up solder method. Pickle and rinse the brooch.

10 Remove all firescale with 400-grit sandpaper, and then give the brooch a final finish. (I used fine-grit steel wool to create a satin finish.)

11 Snip the four wires soldered to the brooch in step 8 until they are each approximately 2 to 3 mm tall.

12 Following the manufacturer's instructions and safety precautions, mix the two-part epoxy resin. Use a wooden toothpick to place a drop of the epoxy in the hole of each half-drilled pearl. To peg set the pearls, affix one to each short length of wire. Let the epoxy dry.

13 Use flat-nose pliers to secure the pin stem in the pin joint.

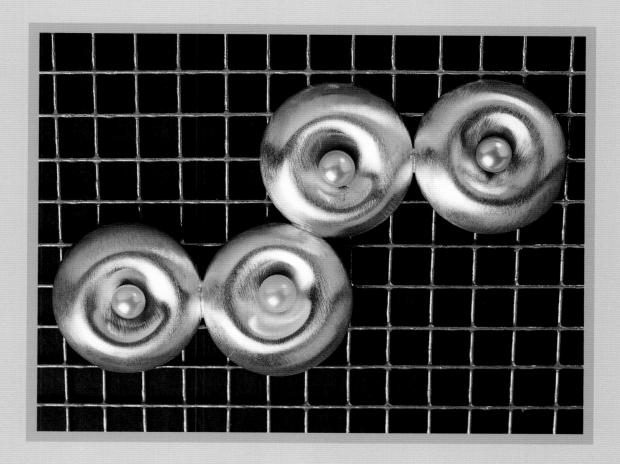

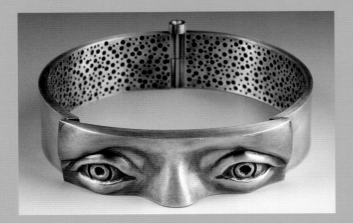

TOP LEFT: Dayna Mae Orione
Fairie, 2003. 16.5 x 6.4 x 3.8 cm. Silver, jasper; repoussé, piercing. Photo © Alan Farkas

TOP RIGHT: Kathleen Browne
Worry, 2004. 28.5 x 17.5 x 0.8 cm. Fine silver, sterling silver, enamels, decals; dapped, fabricated, hand printed, oxidized. Photo © artist

CENTER LEFT: So Young Park
The Moment of Hypocrisy, 2000. Largest, 6 x 9 x 3 cm. Sterling silver, gold leaf; chased, soldered, oxidized. Photo © The Studio Point

CENTER RIGHT: Munya Avigail Upin
Untitled, 2005. 3 x 2.5 x 2.5 cm. Sterling silver, copper; fold formed, micro folded, die formed, fabricated. Photo © artist

BOTTOM LEFT: So Young Park
Thinking Eye, 2000. 12.4 x 12 x 3 cm. Sterling silver; chased, soldered, drilled, oxidized. Photo © The Studio Point

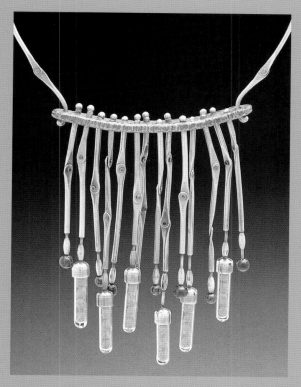

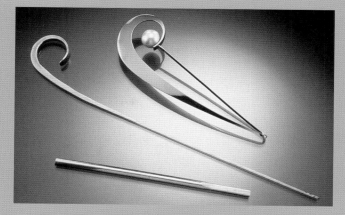

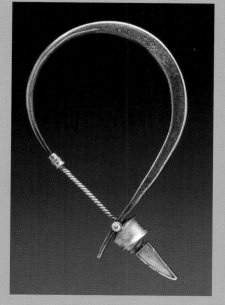

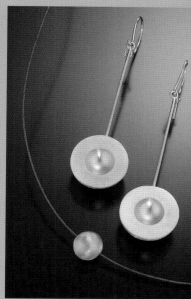

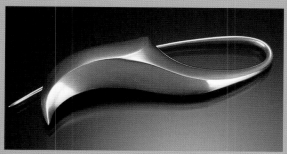

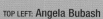

TOP LEFT: Angela Bubash
Segment, 2003. 31.8 x 7 x 2.5 cm. Sterling silver, copper, garnets, yarrow, glass; forged, fabricated. Photo © Tom Mills

TOP RIGHT: Richard Messina
Pearl Plume Pin, 1995. 7.6 x 3.2 cm. 14-karat gold; hand forged, lap polished, finished. Photo © artist

CENTER LEFT: Steven Lubecki
Fibula, 2002. 2 x 6.5 x 1 cm. Sterling silver; forged, chased, repoussé. Photo © Robert Diamante

CENTER MIDDLE: Andy Cooperman
Strung Opal Vertebra, 1998. 7.6 cm. Shibuishi, 14-karat gold, opal; forged, oxidized, fabricated. Photo © Doug Yaple

CENTER RIGHT: Marguerite Chiang Manteau
Cherry & Pit Earrings and Necklace, 2004. Earrings each, 6.4 x 1.9 cm; necklace, 40.6 cm long. 18-karat gold, fishing wire, sterling silver, silver and 18-karat bimetal; hand fabricated. Photo © Hap Sakwa

BOTTOM RIGHT: So Young Park
Nativity Series Brooch and Earrings, 2004. Largest, 5 x 5 x 1 cm. 18-karat gold, sterling silver; dapped, soldered. Photo © Jae Man Jo

Texturing Metal

You can use many different techniques to alter the texture of sheet metal and add interest to your jewelry pieces. Chasing and repoussé are two ways that have already been discussed. Roller printing, reticulation, and etching are other versatile methods. At the end of this chapter, pages 90–93, there are two projects that incorporate these skills.

Roller Printing

For this technique, a rolling mill is used to transfer the texture from another source onto a metal surface through pressure. This process works best on an annealed sheet because the metal is soft and readily accepts the imprint.

MATERIALS
Nonferrous sheet metal of your choice, width trimmed to fit within mill's rollers,* long enough to accommodate design source
Design source (see list below for possible options)
Nonferrous metal top sheet, if needed

TOOLS & SUPPLIES
Soldering kit, page 27
Rolling mill
Wooden or rawhide mallet

Every rolling mill varies in this aspect, so check out the rolling mill you are using prior to cutting the metal to size.

Design Sources for Texture

Lace
Coarse cloth
Dried leaves
Window screen
Mass of tangled wire
Broken saw blades
Etched sheet metal
Pierced and sawed sheet metal

STEP BY STEP

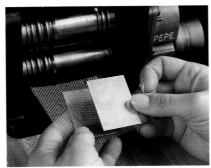

1 Anneal the metal you want to roller print. Lay the design source on top of the metal. If you are using a ferrous metal design source, cover it with a nonferrous metal top sheet to protect the rollers from being imprinted. A top sheet is not necessary if the design source is not metal, although it is good practice to sandwich the design source between two layers of nonferrous metal.

2 Open the rollers on the mill until the metal "sandwich" (the sheets of metal and the design source) fit snugly between the two rollers. Remove the metal from the mill. Move the rollers closer together by turning the handle on the mill one-half revolution. (Depending on how deep an imprint you wish to make and your design source, you may need to experiment with turning the handle more or less than half a turn.)

3 Roll the metal "sandwich" through the mill. The handle should be somewhat difficult but not impossible to turn.

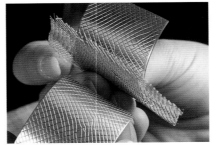

4 Remove the metal from the rolling mill and open the stack to see the imprint. You will probably need to re-anneal the metal sheet and hammer it flat with a wooden or rawhide mallet before using it.

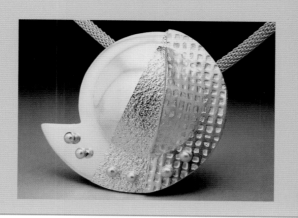

Reticulation

Reticulation uses heat to melt the surface of metal in a controlled manner. This texturing technique is best suited for sterling silver, fine silver, and gold. Brass, copper, bronze, and nickel do not work well.

MATERIALS
Sterling silver, fine silver, or gold sheet metal

TOOLS & SUPPLIES
Pumice or green scrub pad
Soldering kit, page 27

STEP BY STEP

1 Clean the sheet metal with pumice or a green scrub pad until water sheets off the surface. Dry the metal.

2 Place the clean metal on a flat soldering surface. Light the soldering torch and adjust the gas to produce a gentle flame. Begin to heat the metal slowly and evenly.

3 As soon as the metal surface starts to crinkle, move the flame to a new area. You can control the crinkling to some extent by continually moving the flame over the sheet metal, concentrating the heat in one area, and then moving to another area and concentrating the heat there for the same amount of time.

4 Once the desired surface texture has been achieved, pickle, rinse, and dry the metal.

BENCH TIPS

Caution: Overheating the metal will cause it to melt. As you are reticulating, it is easy to burn holes in the sheet, so it is better to remove the heat at the first sign of melting than to take a chance of overheating the metal.

Achieving a perfectly even reticulated surface requires much experimentation and practice. Don't be afraid to test this technique and use it to generate interesting and unusual surface designs.

Several types of sheet metal are made just for reticulating. If you like the technique and plan to use it a lot in your jewelry designs, it may be advantageous to invest in these specially formulated metal sheets.

Etching

The etching process uses a mordant, or acid solution, to eat away metal, leaving a relief design on its surface. This design can be as spontaneous or as precise as desired. A resist material is used to shield areas from being eaten by the acid. Depending on the type of design to be etched, there are many different resists you can use. Popular resists include asphaltum, contact paper, packing tape, electrical tape, adhesive letters or numbers, spray paint, grease pencil, permanent marker, paint pens, shellac, nail polish, and PNP Blue transfer paper (commercially used for etching computer circuit boards).

There are two main mordant formulas for etching metal. The first solution is three parts water to one part nitric acid. Copper, bronze, brass, and nickel can all be etched in the same bath with this solution. Sterling silver will need its own bath, and mild steel will need a separate bath as well. The second solution is composed of four parts water to one part ferric chloride. Copper, brass, bronze, and nickel can all be etched in the same bath with this solution. Aluminum will need its own bath.

Once etched, metal surfaces can be further enhanced with many techniques, including resin inlay, champlevé enameling, patination, and solder inlay. Etched sheets also make an interesting design source for roller printing texture onto another metal sheet.

MATERIALS
Sheet metal of your choice
Resist materials of your choice
Packing tape
Mordant solution of your choice
Baking soda or ammonia and water solution
Mineral spirits or lacquer thinner (optional, depending on resist material)

TOOLS & SUPPLIES
Pumice or green scrub pad
Glass or ceramic container large enough to hold metal
Safety goggles
Rubber gloves
Mask or respirator with correct filter
Apron
Brass brush (optional)

STEP BY STEP

1 Clean the sheet metal with pumice or a scrub pad until water sheets off its surface. Hold the clean metal only by its edges, making certain not to leave any fingerprints on the surface.

2 Completely cover the back surface of the sheet metal with a resist material. (Wide packing tape is the easiest option.)

3 Apply the desired resist to the front surface of the metal. The application method can be additive or subtractive, depending on the resist used. Keep in mind that the area covered with resist will be the raised area on the etched sheet.

4 Following the manufacturer's instructions and safety precautions, mix the mordant solution in the glass or ceramic container. Always add the acid to the water rather than the other way around.

5 Adhere a long piece of packing tape to the back surface of the prepared metal and secure the metal in the acid bath. The front surface of the metal should be touching the top of the acid, just barely submerged and almost floating on top of the acid. (This helps protect the back surface from being etched. The tape on the back also helps you remove the metal from the acid easily.) Gently tap the metal to remove any air bubbles that may have formed underneath the sheet.

6 Check the progress of the etching every 10 to 15 minutes until the desired depth is achieved.

7 Remove the metal from the acid bath and immediately wash it with baking soda or ammonia and water to neutralize the acid (see photo). Scrub the metal with a brass brush or a green scrub pad to make sure all the acid is removed from the metal.

8 Remove the resist material from the metal. (Mineral spirits will remove asphaltum and lacquer thinner will remove PNP Blue transfer paper and paint products.) Clean and dry the etched metal.

9 Add baking soda to the acid bath to neutralize the solution. It will bubble and smoke, so be sure to do this in a sink in a well-ventilated area. Once fully neutralized, the acid can be poured safely down the sink. Wash the container with water and baking soda. (Once used, it must be permanently dedicated for use as an etching bath. Never use the container with food products.)

BENCH TIPS

Always wear protective equipment when working with acid. Goggles, rubber gloves, an apron, and a mask or respirator with the correct filter are required.

Always work in a well-ventilated area or outside when using acids.

If acid comes in contact with your skin, immediately wash it with baking soda and water. If acid comes in contact with your eyes, immediately flush them with water and seek medical attention.

Keep all solvents away from fire and heat.

Roller-Printed Ring

A roller-printed band attached to the surface of a wider, inner band makes this design particularly appealing. For additional contrast, enhance the texture with a black patina.

MATERIALS

Sterling silver rectangular wire, 1 x 6 mm
Sterling silver sheet, 18 gauge
Liver of sulfur
Hot water

TOOLS & SUPPLIES

Bench tool kit, page 27
Soldering kit, page 27
Metal screen or other design source for roller printing
Glass bowl
Rubber gloves
Fine steel wool (optional)

STEP BY STEP

1 Refer to the chart on page 172 to determine the length of metal needed for your ring size. Mark a rectangle on the 18-gauge sterling silver sheet that is 13 mm wide and as long as needed for your ring size. Use the jeweler's saw to cut out the sterling silver rectangle, and then file its edges smooth.

2 Measure and mark a length of the sterling silver rectangular wire that is approximately 3.5 mm longer than the length of your ring size. Use the jeweler's saw to cut the wire length, and then file the cut ends smooth.

3 Roller print the texture of the metal screen (or other design source) onto the rectangular wire, making sure that the action of the rolling mill does not extend the length of the rectangular wire. If the length of your wire does become extended, cut the wire back to size.

4 Bend each of the silver pieces (the sheet and the printed wire) into a circular band. The ends of each band must be perfectly flush. Use hard solder to join the ends of each band, and then pickle and rinse the metal. One at a time, place the bands on a ring mandrel and hammer them into perfect circles.

5 The larger, rectangular-wire band is the ring's outer band. The smaller, silver-sheet band is the ring's inner band. Place the outer band over the inner band and make sure there is a tight fit. If the outer band needs to be larger, place it on the ring mandrel and hammer it with a rawhide mallet to increase its size.

6 File and sand the solder joints on both bands. Each band should look as good as a finished ring.

7 Slide the outer band over the inner band. Adjust the roller-

printed band until it is centered on the inner band. Solder the outer band in place using easy solder, and then pickle and rinse the ring.

8 Sand both the inside and outside of the ring with 400-grit sandpaper to remove all firescale.

9 Place the ring in a liver-of-sulfur solution to give the silver a patina, and then rinse the ring in water. (Refer to page 58 for complete instructions on using liver of sulfur.)

10 Sand the darkened ring with 400-grit sandpaper, making sure to leave the patina in the recessed areas. Give the ring a final finish. (I used fine steel wool to create a satin finish.)

Reticulated Earrings

Reticulated metal has an intense, sculptural texture. In this tasteful earring design, the silver is subtly enhanced with clean wire lines and a graceful shape.

MATERIALS

Sterling silver sheet, 22 gauge
Sterling silver round wire, 14 gauge
Commercial sterling silver ear posts and nuts
Liver of sulfur or selenium toner
Hot water

TOOLS & SUPPLIES

Bench tool kit, page 27
Tape
Photocopied design template, page 172
Soldering kit, page 27
Glass bowl
Heavy-grit steel wool

STEP BY STEP

1 Measure and mark a 1³/4 x 1-inch (4.4 x 2.5 cm) square on the 22-gauge sterling silver sheet. Use the jeweler's saw to cut out the square. Following the process described on page 87, reticulate the silver square.

2 Tape the photocopied template to the reticulated metal to use as a sawing guide. Use the jeweler's saw to cut out the oval shapes.

3 File the edges of the ovals even and smooth.

4 Use the jeweler's saw to cut two lengths of the 14-gauge sterling silver wire, each approximately 3 inches (7.6 cm) long. Use the saw to cut two additional lengths of the 14-gauge wire, each approximately 1 inch (2.5 cm) long.

5 Bend one of the 3-inch (7.6 cm) wire pieces around the outside curve of one of the reticulated silver ovals. The wire must sit directly next to the outer edge of the oval. This requires a lot of manipulation, so remain patient as you bend. Repeat this step for the second silver oval.

6 Using the stick solder method with hard solder, attach each bent wire to the outer edge of a silver oval. Pickle and rinse the metal.

7 Snip any excess wire off the soldered forms, and then sand the wire ends flat.

8 Bend one of the 1-inch (2.5 cm) wire pieces around the inside curve of one of the reticulated silver ovals. The wire must sit directly next to the inner edge of the oval. Repeat this step for the second silver oval.

9 Using the stick solder method with medium solder, attach each bent wire to the inner curve of a silver oval. Pickle and rinse the metal.

10 Snip any excess wire off the forms. File the ends of the inner wires flush with the ends of the outer wires. Sand all wires where they meet.

11 Using the pick-up solder method with easy solder, attach one ear post at the top of the inner curve of each earring. Pickle and rinse the earrings.

12 Apply a black patina to the earrings with liver of sulfur or selenium toner. (Refer to pages 58 and 59 for patina instructions.) Use heavy-grit steel wool to rub the patina off the higher areas of the reticulated silver and to polish the round wire.

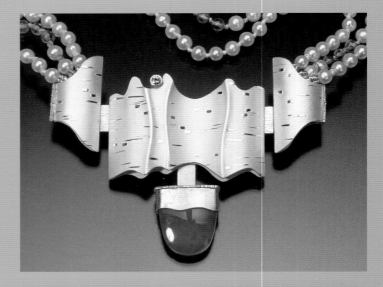

TOP LEFT: Sadie Shu Ping Wang
Silver Brooch, 2002. 7.9 x 5.4 x 1.3 cm. Sterling silver, resin, citrine; fabricated, set, reticulated. Photo © Azad Photo

TOP RIGHT: Joan Tenenbaum
Birch Forest Necklace II, 2003. Pendant, 5.1 x 6.7 x 3.2 cm; chain, 45.7 cm long. 18-karat gold, sterling silver, chrysoprase, blue diamond, freshwater pearls, apatite beads, silk; roller printed, fold formed, hand textured, hand fabricated. Photo © Doug Yaple

CENTER LEFT: Taweesak Molsawat
What Do You Think?, 2004. 26.7 x 19 x 0.3 cm. Sterling silver; etched, hand fabricated. Photo © artist

CENTER RIGHT: Junghyun Woo
White Christmas, 2001. 23 x 23 x 23 cm. Copper, fine silver, cubic zirconia, monofilament; etched, plated, set. Photo © Helen Shirk

BOTTOM LEFT: Natalya Pinchuk
Building Rings, 2001. Largest, 7 x 2.5 x 2.5 cm. Sterling silver, 18-karat gold solder, avonite; hand fabricated, etched, riveted, oxidized. Photo © artist

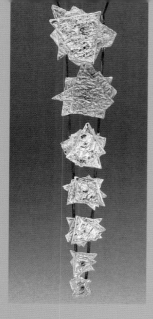

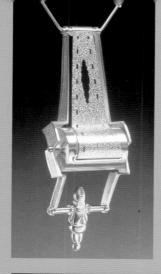

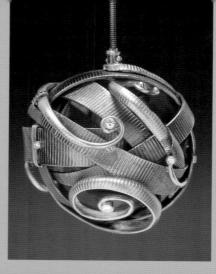

TOP LEFT: Chie Nakai
Rain in the City, 2005. 60 cm long. Silver, copper tubing, wire; reticulated, riveted, beaded. Photo © David Butler

TOP CENTER: Pamela Morris Thomford
Tripping to Tim's to Record a Fact, 1996. Pendant, 13.8 x 5 x 3 cm; chain, 50 cm long. Sterling silver; hand fabricated, roller printed, cast. Photo © Tim Thayer

TOP RIGHT: Andy Cooperman
Medusa, 2001. 4.4 cm in diameter. Sterling silver, 18-karat gold, diamonds, guitar wire. Photo © Doug Yaple

CENTER LEFT: Estelle Renée Vernon
Japanese Textile Series: Petals Brooch, 2005. 7.1 x 2.2 x 0.7 cm. Copper and fine silver bimetal, sterling silver, patina; hand fabricated, etched, die formed. Photo © Robert Diamante

CENTER RIGHT: Marguerite Chiang Manteau
Garland Necklace, 2004. 40.6 x 3.8 x 3.8 cm. Sterling silver; fold formed, roller printed, hand fabricated. Photo © Hap Sakwa

BOTTOM RIGHT: Nina Mann
Earrings 22KY-Ruby, 2004. Each, 1 x 1 x 0.2 cm. Shibuishi, 22-karat yellow gold; amalgamated, reticulated, molded in sheet form, cast, fabricated. Photo © Ralph Gabriner

Layering Metals

Using layering techniques as diverse as appliqué, granulation, filigree, and kum boo will allow you to introduce depth, texture, pattern, and color to your jewelry designs. You can practice your appliqué and filigree skills in two projects at the end of this chapter on pages 110–113.

Appliqué

Appliqué is a layering technique in which one piece of sheet metal is soldered on top of another piece of sheet metal. This process has many applications.

MATERIALS
- Sheet metal of your choice (base for appliqué)
- Sheet metal of your choice, 18 to 26 gauge (for appliqué)

TOOLS & SUPPLIES
- Bench tool kit, page 27
- Soldering kit, page 27

STEP BY STEP

1 Prepare the base piece of metal by sawing out the form or fabricating the structure you have planned for your design. Sand the prepared base to a 400-grit finish.

2 Design and draw the appliqué shapes on the 18- to 26-gauge sheet metal. Saw out the appliqués, and smooth their edges with needle files. Sand the bottom of each appliqué to a 400-grit finish.

3 Place the appliqués on the soldering block with the bottom (sanded side) facing up. Flux the bottom side of each appliqué.

4 Cut solder snippets from a piece of easy solder, each approximately 2 mm long. (I recommend using as little solder as possible for this process so that excess solder won't run out from under the appliqué.) If you have tiny appliqué pieces, then use smaller solder snippets.

5 Use a solder pick to transfer one or two easy-solder snippets to each appliqué piece. Light the torch and use the heat to melt the solder onto each appliqué. While it is still hot and viscous, smear the solder across each appliqué with the solder pick (see photo). Cover as much surface area as possible with a thin film of solder without melting the appliqué.

6 Pickle and rinse all appliqué pieces. Flux the prepared metal base in the areas where the appliqués will be applied and flux the back of each appliqué.

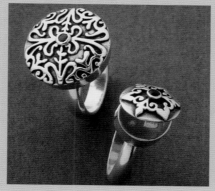

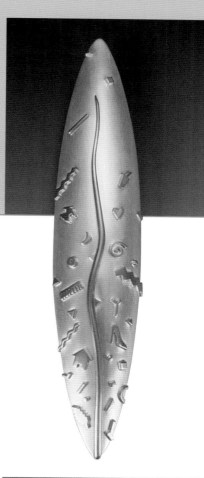

7 At this point, you have two options: either heat the flux on the base piece until it is glassy, stop heating the metal, and place the fluxed appliqué pieces on the metal; or position the appliqué pieces on the base sheet, and then gently heat the piece. With either option there is a chance that the appliqués will move around the base piece when the flux becomes fluid. If the appliqués do move, gently reposition them with the solder pick while continuing to heat the piece. No matter which method you choose, heat the piece, concentrating the heat on the base, and then gently run the flame over the appliqué pieces (see photo). The goal is to heat each piece of metal to the same temperature so they will solder together easily without melting the appliqués.

8 When the metal is hot enough, concentrate the heat on a single appliqué, making sure the solder flows all the way around its edges. A bright line of wet solder should appear all the way around the edges of the appliqué. Once the bright line is visible, immediately stop heating the appliqué and move the torch flame onto the next appliqué. Continue this process until all of the appliqués are completely soldered onto the base. Pickle and rinse the piece.

BENCH TIP

When soldering the appliqués to the base, I prefer to heat the piece from above. This position allows me to add appliqués to many different types of base forms. Some people prefer to heat the metal from underneath the piece. If you are soldering appliqués onto a hollow form, however, heating from underneath will not work, so I encourage you to become proficient at soldering from above.

Granulation

In the ancient technique of granulation, small balls, or
granules, of metal are fused onto a base sheet of metal to create
an intricately patterned design. Although fine silver and high-
karat golds are easiest to work with and show the beauty of this
process best, sterling silver and other gold alloys can also be
used. There are several steps involved in granulation, including
making the granules, preparing the glue, positioning the design,
preparing the eutectic solder, and finally, firing the granules
with a torch or kiln.

Making a Small Amount of Granules

MATERIALS

Fine silver or 22-karat gold wire,
28 to 30 gauge

TOOLS & SUPPLIES

Very small mandrel, such as 1-mm
piano wire
Embroidery scissors (if needed, file
the ends to fit into smaller spaces)
Charcoal block
Small, sharp hand tool
Soldering torch
Glass or ceramic bowl

STEP BY STEP

1 Wrap the thin wire around
the very small mandrel.
Each revolution around the mandrel equals one granule. Once
you have made a coil of the
appropriate length for the number of granules needed, slide the
coil off the mandrel.

2 Use your fingers to pull the
coil apart gently, making
enough room for the embroidery
scissors to fit between each loop.
Snip each loop apart from the next
so you have, in essence, created a
pile of very tiny jump rings.

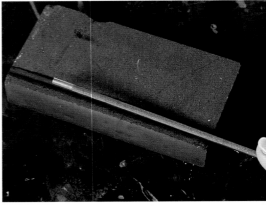

3 Because the next task is messy,
I suggest doing it outdoors.
Carve a groove around the edges of
the charcoal block with any small,
sharp hand tool. This groove prevents the granules from rolling off
the block when they are melted.

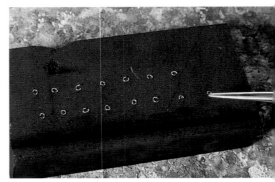

4 Place the cut wire loops on
the charcoal block, leaving
approximately ⅛ inch (3 mm)
between each loop. This space
deters the granules from rolling
into each other and becoming
larger granules when melted.

Making a Large Amount of Granules

MATERIALS
Fine silver or 22-karat gold wire,
28 to 30 gauge
Powdered charcoal

TOOLS & SUPPLIES
Assorted mandrels
Embroidery scissors
Glass or ceramic bowl
Crucible
Kiln
Tongs
Spoon
Soft cloth

STEP BY STEP

1 Repeat steps 1 and 2 from Making a Small Amount of Granules. Use a larger mandrel if larger granules are desired.

2 Wet the wire loops with a few drops of water and mix them into the powdered charcoal in a bowl. This forms a thin layer of charcoal around each loop, and prevents them from sticking together when heated.

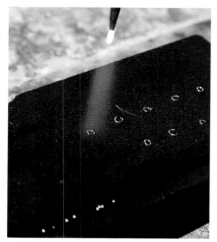

5 Light the torch and adjust the flame so it is bushy and medium size. (A small, tight, hot flame gives out too much pressure and will make the granules roll around the charcoal block.) Gently begin melting the coils into granules with the torch.

6 When all the granules are formed, gently load them into a bowl. Repeat steps 1 through 5 to make different size granules (see Bench Tip).

BENCH TIP

Three sizes of granules can be made using one coil and a single mandrel. Simply cut one, two, or three loops off the coil at a time, and then sort the loops into corresponding piles.

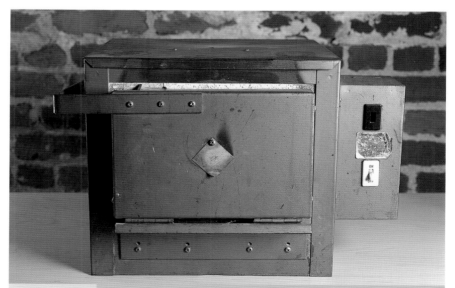

New Tool *A kiln is a brick-lined oven used for melting metal and for firing enamels and metal clay. It is heat resistant on the outside but can reach and maintain extremely high temperatures on the inside.*

Placing & Fusing the Granules

Prior to fusing the granules to the metal base, it is necessary to mix two solutions. The first, a hide glue and water mixture, helps adhere the granules in position. The second, a copper hydroxide solution, facilitates the fusing process.

MATERIALS
Metal sheet for base
Hide glue mixture (formula, page 101)
Granules
Copper hydroxide solution (formula, page 101)

TOOLS & SUPPLIES
Pumice or green scrub pad
Small paintbrush
Small tweezers
Paper towels
Small, natural-hair paintbrush
Soldering kit, page 27

STEP BY STEP

Placing the Granules

3 Place a layer of charcoal-covered wire loops in the crucible. Add approximately ¼ inch (6 mm) of charcoal on top of the loops. Repeat this process, alternating loops and charcoal, until the crucible is full.

4 Fire the crucible in a kiln until the crucible is red hot, and then remove the crucible from the kiln with tongs (see photo). Remove a few of the metal pieces from the crucible with a spoon and drop them into a bowl of water. If the metal pieces have formed into round granules, you are finished. If not, place the crucible back in the kiln and refire.

5 Once the granules are fully formed, rinse them, and then dry them with a soft cloth.

1 Completely clean the metal sheet with pumice or a green scrub pad until water sheets off its surface. Hold the clean metal by its edges to avoid fingerprints.

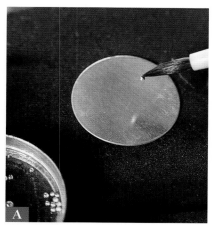

A

B

2   Dip the paintbrush into the hide glue mixture. Use the wet brush to pick up the granules and place them on the base sheet (photo A). If it is easier, use small tweezers to pick up and place the granules, dipping them into the hide glue mixture as you go (photo B).

3   If there is too much liquid accumulating on the base sheet and the granules begin to move around, roll up the edge of a paper towel and gently place it near the liquid. The paper towel will wick up the liquid without disturbing the granule placement. Do not allow the hide glue mixture to dry before adding the copper hydroxide solution to the granules (step 4). If the glue mixture dries, simply add more with the paintbrush.

Formulas

Hide Glue Mixture
1 part hide glue
10 parts water

Copper Hydroxide Solution for Silver
1 heaping part copper hydroxide ($Cu(OH)2$)*
2 to 5 parts diluted hide glue (see formula above)
2 to 3 drops high-temperature liquid flux

For silver, the copper hydroxide must be at least 65 to 85 percent pure, but compounds with a higher purity will also work.

Copper Hydroxide Solution for Gold
1 heaping part copper hydroxide ($Cu(OH)2$)*
2 to 4 parts diluted hide glue (see formula above)
2 to 3 drops high-temperature liquid flux

For gold, the copper hydroxide must be at least 85 to 95 percent pure.

Important Note: Copper hydroxide is not water-soluble. During application, the mixture must be constantly stirred to make sure the copper hydroxide is evenly distributed throughout the solution.

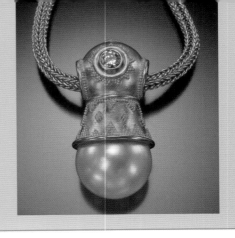

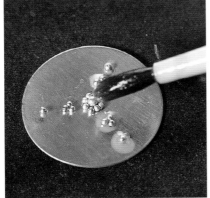

4 Using a small, natural-hair paintbrush, add the copper hydroxide solution to the granules that are in position (see photo). Make sure the solution settles at the bottom of the granules. Remove any excess solution from the granules with a paper towel. This is very important—wherever there is copper hydroxide and glue together, the metal surface will melt when heated, causing unsightly blotches. Clean up all mistakes with the paintbrush or a paper towel.

5 Set the piece aside and allow the glue mixture to dry completely. If you have a kiln, you can set the piece on top of it to dry faster. Do not attempt to dry the piece with the torch, because that will cause the water to spit and the granules to move or even fly off the piece.

Fusing the Granules

6 Place the dry piece on a soldering block. Use a torch with a soft, but hot bushy flame to heat the piece until the glue mixture turns brown. (A very hot flame is too scorching, and a tight flame could disturb the granules.)

7 Continue to heat the piece very slowly until it begins to look silver or gold again. Heat around the granulation design, and then every once in a while gently run the flame over the design. Do not rush this process.

8 As the piece approaches granulating temperature, the areas where copper hydroxide was added will glow red. Once these areas turn orange, look for a silver or gold flash. When the surface of the metal begins to shimmer and look watery, gently stroke the torch over each granulated area. This stroke is not a direct heating, but more of a pause right over the granules. This step fuses the granules to

the base sheet, so it is very important. The granulation bonds, however, do not form instantly. The piece must be held at the granulating temperature for a few seconds. Do not overheat the piece, because the granules could melt into the base and lose their shape.

9 Remove the heat and let the piece air cool. Do not quench or pickle it.

Finishing a Granulated Piece

10 Use tweezers to check the granules. If any are loose and did not fuse, repeat this process from the beginning. You can refire the piece two or three times without pickling. Once all the granules are fused, pickle and rinse the piece.

11 After pickling, it is best simply to rub the piece with a fine-bristle brass brush to give it some shine (see photo). Do not attempt to use any kind of pol-ish on the piece except for rouge compound. Polishing with a coarser compound will diminish the roundness of the granules and the piece will appear dull and flat. If you choose to use rouge com-pound, do not hold the piece too firmly against the polishing wheel. Be gentle and let the wheel do the work, and constantly check to make sure the granules are retain-ing their integrity.

Filigree

In filigree, an ancient technique that has been used by many cultures throughout the world, tiny wires are used to create extremely intricate designs. Closed filigree is formed on top of a metal base, whereas open filigree has no backing and you can see through the design.

An assortment of filigree wire shapes and balls

The decorative wires can be made into any shape, and then arranged into countless different forms. Small wires can be twisted together before they are shaped. Standard round wire can be used, or square wire can be twisted with a round wire. This process offers the opportunity to be very creative. Feel free to invent as many interesting kinds of wire shapes and patterns as you can imagine.

Making Dry Flux

The filigree technique requires the use of dry, powdered flux. Here's how to make your own.

MATERIALS
Standard paste flux

TOOLS & SUPPLIES
Aluminum foil or glass baking dish
Oven (optional)
Mortar and pestle
Lidded storage container for excess dry flux (optional)
Shaker, such as a salt and pepper shaker

STEP BY STEP

1 Scoop out standard paste flux from the jar. Smear the paste flux onto the aluminum foil or baking dish. Set the foil or dish in the sun or place it in an oven on low heat until the flux is completely dry.

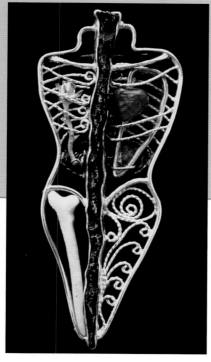

Creating Closed Filigree

MATERIALS

Sheet metal of your choice,
18 gauge or thinner
Wire of your choice,
18 gauge or thinner
Liquid or paste flux
Liquid hide glue solution (optional,
see formula on page 101)
Powdered flux in shaker
Granules (optional)

TOOLS & SUPPLIES

Bench tool kit, page 27
Pumice or green scrub pad
Soldering kit, page 27
Glass or ceramic bowl
Fine-nose tweezers
Paper towels
Brass brush

3 In a bowl, make a flux and water mixture that is mostly water with a tiny bit of liquid or paste flux (see photo), or use a liquid hide glue solution. This mixture helps adhere the filigree elements to the base temporarily.

STEP BY STEP

1 Design and fabricate the metal base on which the filigree will be constructed. Clean the base with pumice or a scrub pad and place it on the soldering block.

2 Design the closed filigree embellishment on paper, and then cut and form the wires as needed to realize the design. (As you make the wire forms, it may be helpful to position them on top of the drawn design as a reference.)

2 Place a small amount of the dry flux in the mortar, and use the pestle to grind the flux into a very fine powder. (Store the remainder of the dry flux in a separate container until you are ready to use it, or continue to grind the rest in small batches.) Place the powdered flux in a salt or pepper shaker for immediate use.

4 Using fine-nose tweezers, pick up one filigree element, dip it into the flux and water or glue solution, and then place it on the metal base. Continue adding the filigree elements until the design is complete. If the base becomes too wet with excess glue, gently use the twisted corner of a paper towel to soak up excess moisture.

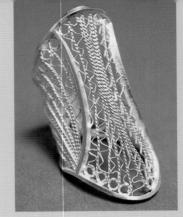

5 Allow the fixative to dry completely. You can place the piece on top of a heater or an oven to speed this process. (Any residual moisture could cause wire elements to dislodge from the base when it is heated with the torch in step 6.)

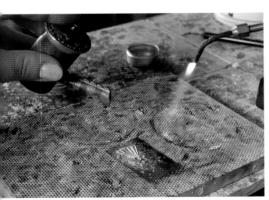

6 Light the torch and adjust the flame so it is bushy and soft. Begin gently heating the metal with the flame. When the piece is hot enough that the fixative melts, sprinkle some dry flux onto the metal (see photo). Let this flux melt in the heat of the flame, and then add more flux and melt it. Repeat this process. Two or three additions of flux are usually sufficient, but you can add more if needed. The metal should appear glassy-green or glassy-blue based on the amount of flux on the piece.

7 All of the soldering for a simple filigree piece can be accomplished in one heating. Heat the piece until the flux appears glassy as in step 6, and then gently touch a medium solder stick to each wire element. Only touch the solder to the wires, not to the metal base. Make sure you see a bright line of solder under and around each and every wire element. Twisted wires require more solder than straight wires do. Pickle and rinse the piece.

8 Use a brass brush to shine the filigree and make sure all the wire elements are securely soldered. If all the wires are not soldered down, repeat steps 6 and 7.

9 If you wish to add granules (balls) to the filigree, simply repeat steps 4 through 8 using granules instead of wires.

Creating Open Filigree

STEP BY STEP

1 Form the wire elements for an open filigree design by following step 2 of Creating Closed Filigree.

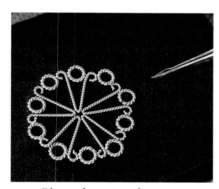

2 Place the wire elements on a compressed charcoal block. Adjust the position of the wires as needed so all elements are touching an adjacent element. This is the latticework of the open filigree.

3 Heat the wire elements and add dry flux from the shaker.

4 Solder the wires with medium stick solder, and then pickle and rinse the piece. Use a brass brush to shine the filigree and make sure all the wires are securely soldered.

BENCH TIPS

Use very small wires for an extremely intricate open filigree piece. Use larger wires for a more substantial-looking design.

Once you create a latticework of open filigree, try forming it in a dapping block or around a mandrel.

LEFT: **Jacquelyn A. Crissman**
Reading the Wind, 2004. 11.5 x 7 x 2.5 cm.
Sterling silver, fine silver, 24-karat gold, nickel silver,
goose feathers; fabricated, kum boo, roller printed,
twined. Photos © Ericka Crissman, Wired Images

RIGHT: **Marguerite Chiang Manteau**
Pan Flute Bracelet, 2004. 16.5 x 5.1 cm. Sterling
silver, 24-karat gold, 18-karat gold; kum boo, hand
fabricated, file finished. Photo © Hap Sakwa

FAR RIGHT: **Liana Patsuria**
Untitled, 2004. 5.3 x 6.7 x 0.7 cm. Silver, 22-karat
gold; hand fabricated, kum boo. Photo © Ligia Botero

Kum Boo

In this traditional Korean technique, also known as keum bu, thin gold foil is bonded to another metal, most often fine or sterling silver. Low heat, such as a hot plate set at 650°F (343.3°C), is used to activate the bond. The foil can be applied before and after the metal is formed into a jewelry piece.

Kum boo utilizes a joining method known as pressure welding. First, the two metals are heated to a temperature where no oxygen is present between them. Next, the pressure of a burnisher is applied to the foil. Finally, the two metals are permanently bonded in a low-temperature, thin-molecular weld.

MATERIALS

22-karat gold foil, approximately 0.004 mm thick (not enameling foil)
Sheet metal or jewelry piece of your choice, fine or sterling silver

TOOLS & SUPPLIES

Small embroidery scissors or decorative hole punches
Paper (optional)
Tape (optional)
Small clean dish
Hot plate
Steel plate to fit hot plate, approximately 1 mm thick
Brass brush, if using sterling silver
Pumice
Tweezers
Small clean paintbrush
Polished burnisher
Straight pin

STEP BY STEP

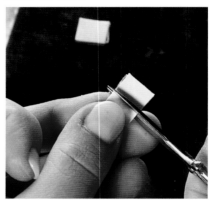

1 Plan your design and the shape of the foil to be added to the silver. Use embroidery scissors or decorative hole punches to cut the foil into the desired shapes. (Before cutting, I suggest sandwiching the foil between two pieces of paper that are taped together. This allows you to cut the foil shape more easily without it floating away or becoming misshapen.) Place the cut foil shapes in a small dish next to your work area.

2 Turn on the hot plate and adjust its setting to a medium-high temperature. (You may need to experiment to see exactly how hot the plate gets at certain settings, and you may want to record this information for future use.) Place the thin steel plate on the hot plate. The steel plate helps the heat spread evenly throughout the base metal form. It also prevents small metal forms from falling through the hot plate burners.

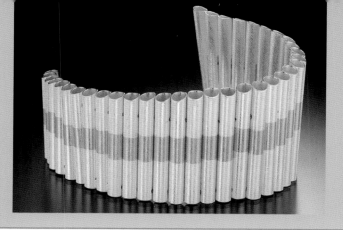

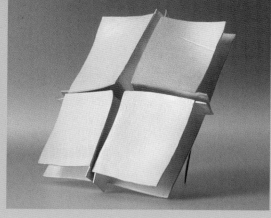

3 If you are using a sterling silver base form, raise the fine silver to the surface (refer to pages 49–50 for instructions). Brass brush, and then completely clean the metal. If you are using a fine silver base form, simply clean the piece completely.

4 Place the metal base form on the preheated steel plate. Let the form warm to the hot plate's temperature.

5 Pick up a cut foil shape with tweezers or with a wet paintbrush, whichever works best for you, and position the foil on the metal base form.

6 Use the burnisher to press the foil into place. If the metal base is hot enough, the foil will easily stick to the base metal piece, and you can continue burnishing by quickly and lightly rubbing the foil with smooth strokes. You don't need to press very hard. If the metal is not hot enough, the foil won't stick to the base form. If this happens, either increase the temperature of the hot plate or wait until the base form gets hotter.

7 Repeat steps 5 and 6 until all of the gold foil is in place. If any of the foil bubbles up, simply re-burnish it. If there is a large bubble in the foil, poke it with a straight pin to let the air out, and then re-burnish it.

Note: If the base form gets too hot, the gold foil can diffuse into the silver, dulling the color of the foil and weakening the kum boo effect. If this happens, either lower the temperature of the hot plate or remove the base form from the hot plate for a moment to let it cool down, and then add more foil to the effected area. You can also add a drop of water to the overheated area to help it cool down as long as the water does not come between the gold foil and the silver base.

8 Finish the metal piece. A black patina looks great with kum boo, as it will not affect the gold foil. When using kum boo, a high polish is not as desirable as a matte finish; the high polish will mask the color difference between the gold and the silver. If you intend to use a polishing machine, however, do so with great care.

Appliquéd Orb Bracelet

Simple metal circles of contrasting colors and sizes are appliquéd onto sterling silver to form an imaginative and eye-catching design. This project is easy to adapt, so experiment with different appliqué shapes, arrangements, and metal choices.

MATERIALS
Sterling silver flat wire, 1 x 4 mm
Sterling silver sheet, 18 gauge
Brass sheet, 24 gauge
Sterling silver sheet, 24 gauge

TOOLS & SUPPLIES
Bench tool kit, page 27
Soldering kit, page 27

STEP BY STEP

1 Use the jeweler's saw to cut a 6^1/$_4$-inch (15.9 cm) length of the 1 x 4-mm flat wire. Round the ends of the cut wire with the bastard file.

2 Measure and mark a 2 x 5-cm rectangle on the 18-gauge sterling silver sheet. Use the jeweler's saw to cut out the marked rectangle, and then slightly round its edges with the bastard file.

3 Measure and mark a total of six circles on the 24-gauge brass sheet. Make three of the circles ^{1}/$_2$ inch (1.3 cm) in diameter and three of the circles ^{5}/$_8$ inch (1.6 cm) in diameter. Use the jeweler's saw to cut out the marked circles, and then file their edges with a bastard file. Sand the bottom of each circle to a 400-grit finish.

4 Measure and mark a total of six circles on the 24-gauge sterling silver sheet. Make one circle ^{5}/$_8$ inch (1.6 cm) in diameter, three circles ^{1}/$_4$ inch (6 mm) in diameter, and two circles ^{3}/$_8$ inch (1 cm) in diameter. Use the jeweler's saw to cut out the marked circles, and then file their edges with a bastard file. Sand the bottom of each circle to a 400-grit finish.

5 Coat the back of each of the brass and silver circles with flux, and then apply hard solder to cover each circle completely. (Refer to page 96 for complete instructions on this phase of the appliqué process.) Pickle and rinse the circles.

6 Following the appliqué technique described on pages 96–97, solder one small silver circle on top of each of the larger brass circles. Pickle and rinse each circle appliqué.

7 Apply a full layer of flux to the front of the silver rectangle cut in step 2. Arrange the circle appliqués on top of the rectangle in a design that appeals to you. (If desired, you can extend appliqués past the edge of the rectangle; the extra metal can be sawed off later.) Using medium solder, solder the circles to the silver rectangle, and then pickle and rinse the appliquéd piece.

8 Use a jeweler's saw to cut off any extra metal hanging past the edges of the appliquéd rectangle. File and sand the edges of the rectangle smooth.

9 Using a rawhide mallet, gently bend the appliquéd rectangle around a large mandrel to form a soft curve.

10 Using your fingers, bend the flat silver wire cut in step 1 into an oval shape that fits your wrist. Form the center of the oval-shaped wire to match the curve of the appliquéd rectangle.

11 Flux the back of the curved appliquéd rectangle and the top of the curved flat wire. Assemble these components so the flat wire is centered under the rectangle, and use cross-locking tweezers to hold the wire in place. Using the stick solder method with easy solder, attach the flat wire to the rectangle. Pickle and rinse the bracelet.

12 Remove any firescale from the bracelet, and then give the piece a final finish. (I used a green kitchen scrub to create a matte finish.)

Filigree Pendant

Filigree jewelry is always alluring and expressive. Use this closed-filigree pendant to develop your skills, and then design and create original patterns that convey your individuality.

MATERIALS

Sterling silver round wire, 22 gauge
Sterling silver round wire, 20 gauge
Fine silver round wire, 24 gauge
Sterling silver sheet, 24 gauge
Commercial chain of your choice
6 garnet beads or beads of
    your choice, 4 mm
Liver of sulfur or selenium toner
Hot water

TOOLS & SUPPLIES

Bench tool kit, page 27
Small mandrels, 3 mm, 4 mm,
    and 7 mm in diameter
Soldering kit, page 27
Photocopied design template,
    page 172
Glass bowl
Heavy-grit steel wool

STEP BY STEP

1 Cut two 12-inch (30.5 cm) pieces of the 22-gauge sterling silver wire and two 12-inch (30.5 cm) pieces of the 20-gauge sterling silver wire. Twist together the two 22-gauge wire lengths, and then twist together the two 20-gauge wire lengths.

2 Snip four sections of the 20-gauge twisted silver wire, each approximately 1 inch (2.5 cm) long. Bend each of these wire sections around a 4-mm mandrel to make four closed-U shapes.

3 Wrap the 22-gauge twisted silver wire around a 4-mm mandrel to make six jump rings. Saw the jump rings apart, and then close the jump rings.

4 Wrap the 22-gauge twisted silver wire around a 7-mm mandrel to make five jump rings. Saw the jump rings apart, and close them.

5 Using the 7-mm mandrel, make one jump ring from the 20-gauge twisted silver wire. Saw and close the jump ring.

6 Wrap the 24-gauge fine silver wire around a 3-mm mandrel to make five plain jump rings. Saw the jump rings apart and close them.

7 Measure and mark a piece of 24-gauge sterling silver sheet that is large enough to be the backing sheet for the filigree design (approximately 2 x 1½ inches [5.1 x 3.8 cm]). Use the jeweler's saw to cut out this backing sheet.

8 Apply a layer of flux over the entire backing sheet. Using the design template as a guide, arrange all of the jump rings and closed-U-shaped pieces on top of the backing sheet. Lightly dip each wire into the flux before placing it in position. Using the stick solder method and hard solder, attach the wire elements to the silver sheet. Pickle and rinse the piece.

9 To make the balls for the design, wrap the 24-gauge fine silver wire around the 4-mm mandrel approximately 16 times. Saw the jump rings apart. Place two jump rings together on a charcoal block, and melt them into a ball. Repeat this process to make a total

twisted silver wire. (Complete instructions for this process are given on pages 156–157.)

13 Use the 4-mm mandrel and the 20-gauge wire to make four jump rings. Attach one jump ring to the clasp, one to the hook, and one to each of the top two holes in the pendant.

14 Use snips to cut two lengths of the commercial chain, each approximately 7 inches (17.8 cm) long. Attach the chain lengths to the jump rings on the clasp and the pendant, and solder each of the jump rings closed with easy solder. Pickle and rinse the necklace.

15 Use the jeweler's saw to cut six lengths of the 24-gauge fine silver wire, each approximately 2 to 3 inches (5.1 to 7.6 cm) long. Use the torch to melt one end of each wire into a ball. Thread one 4-mm garnet bead onto each wire. Attach two of the wires with garnet beads to each of the three holes at the bottom of the pendant. Secure each wire by forming a loop and then wrapping the wire around itself. Snip off any extra wire.

of five small silver balls. To make the large silver ball, place six jump rings together on the block and melt them.

10 Dip each silver ball into the flux and add it to the filigree design. Stick solder the balls in place with hard solder. Pickle and rinse the piece.

11 Using the design template as your guide, pierce and saw out the negative spaces inside the design, and saw out the outer contour of the pendant. Sand all interior and exterior edges of the pendant smooth.

12 Make an S hook and a clasp from the 22-gauge

16 Give the pendant a black patina, and then rub the whole piece with heavy-grit steel wool to polish the higher parts of the metal.

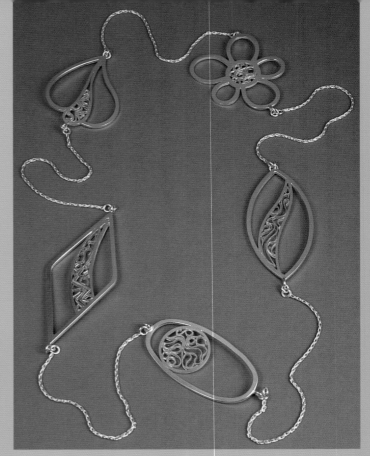

TOP LEFT: Felicity Peters
Necklace—Hand Held Heart Loved (detail), 2001. Each segment, 2.3 x 2.3 x 0.4 cm. 24-karat gold, sterling silver, diamonds, colite; kum boo, stamped, hand fabricated. Photo © Victor France

TOP RIGHT: Munya Avigail Upin
Seasons Plus One, 2005. 6 x 4 x 0.2 cm. Sterling silver, fine silver; filigree, fabricated. Photo © artist

BOTTOM LEFT: Eileen Gerstein
Untitled Kum Boo Necklace, 2000. Focal elements, 5 x 14 x 0.7 cm; chain, 35 cm long. Fine silver, sterling silver, 22-karat gold bimetal, 24-karat gold; hand fabricated, hollow formed, woven, oxidized. Photo © Hap Sakwa

BOTTOM RIGHT: Maija Neimanis
Queen Bee with Diamond Eyes and South Sea Pearl with Granulated Cap, 1994. 5.8 x 5 x 1.4 cm. 22-karat gold, pearl, diamonds; hand fabricated, granulation, repoussé. Photo © Ralph Gabriner

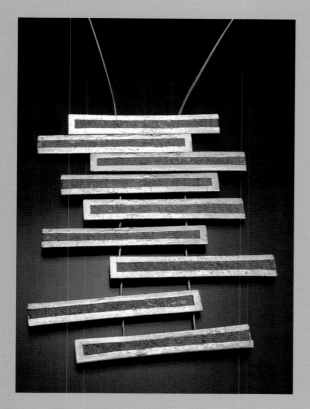

TOP LEFT: **Seth Papac**
Horizontal/Vertical, 2004. 11 x 10 x 10 cm. 18-karat green gold, fine silver, sterling silver; granulation, hand fabricated. Photo © Maria Phillips

TOP RIGHT: **Marguerite Chiang Manteau**
Sun Spiral Neckpiece, 2003. 21.6 x 13.3 cm. Sterling silver, 24-karat gold, 14-karat gold, 18-karat gold; kum boo, hand fabricated, file finished. Photo © Hap Sakwa

BOTTOM LEFT: **Nanz Aalund**
The Sun: Two-Finger Ring (To Be Worn on the First Finger and Pinky Finger), 2004. 4.4 x 8.5 x 2.2 cm. 18-karat gold, stainless steel; filigree, hand fabricated, pierced, laser welded. Photo © Doug Yaple

BOTTOM RIGHT: **Sherry Cordova**
Fraternal Triplets: Carousel, Cordoban, Sri Lankan, 2005. Largest, 3.3 x 3.3 x 1.5 cm. Sterling silver, fine silver, amethyst, garnet, peridot; hand fabricated, filigree. Photo © artist

TOP LEFT: **Charles Lewton-Brain**
Heart Pin, 1997. 5 x 4.5 x 2 cm. Sterling silver, 24-karat gold, paper; kum boo, die printed, hydraulic die formed. Photo © artist

TOP RIGHT: **Felicity Peters**
Tibetan Journey Necklace, 2000. Each element, 5 x 5 x 0.7 cm. 24-karat gold, sterling silver; kum boo. Photo © Victor France

CENTER LEFT: **Joan Tenenbaum**
From River to Sea Necklace, 2004. Pendant, 4.5 x 3.2 x 0.8 cm; Necklace, 45.7 cm long. 18-karat green gold, 18-karat yellow gold, 18-karat palladium white gold, aquamarine; granulation, hand fabricated, riveted. Chain hand knitted by Julia Lowther. Photo © Doug Yaple

BOTTOM LEFT: **Jane Garibaldi**
Bug, 2005. 6.4 x 6.4 x 1.2 cm. Sterling silver, 24-karat gold, turquoise, peridot, apatite, pearl; kum boo, fabricated, roller printed. Photo © Hap Sakwa

BOTTOM RIGHT: **Felicity Peters**
Brooches—House Journeys, 2004. Each, 4.5 x 4 x 0.3 cm. 24-karat gold, sterling silver; granulation, kum boo, roller printed. Photo © Victor France

Mixing Metals

Using contrasting metals in a single jewelry piece can increase its visual intensity. Three popular techniques for mixing metals are marriage of metal, mokume gane, and solder inlay. At the end of the chapter, on pages 126–129, are two projects that incorporate marriage of metal and solder inlay.

Marriage of Metal

The marriage of metal technique produces a multicolored metal design. It is not a surface treatment, but rather a puzzle-like method of assembling metals of different colors. Brass, copper, nickel, silver, and shakudo are all excellent choices for making metal jewelry that incorporates this process.

The inlay technique for marriage of metal uses a design with positive and negative spaces and two or more types of metal with different colors. One metal is used to fill in the negative space on another metal. Because this process uses solder to hold the metal in place, instead of the traditional undercut from a graver, some people may call it a type of inlay.

A second marriage of metal method uses strips or shapes of different colors of sheet metal. The pieces are arranged side by side and soldered together to create a pattern.

Inlay Technique for Marriage of Metal

MATERIALS
2 nonferrous sheet metals of your choice, each 22 gauge

TOOLS & SUPPLIES
Bench tool kit, page 27
Soldering kit, page 27

STEP BY STEP

1 Determine which color of sheet metal to use as the base and which to use as the inlay. (I suggest beginners use a base piece that is no larger than 2 x 2 inches [5.1 x 5.1 cm] because a larger metal sheet can warp and move when heated.) Draw or transfer an inlay design onto the base sheet metal.

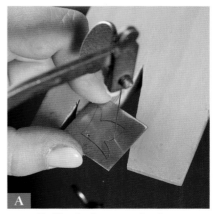

2 Drill a hole near the inner edge of the inlay design. Use a jeweler's saw to cut out the design, forming the negative space for the inlay (photo A). File or

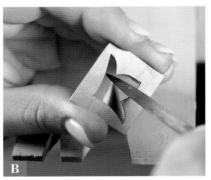

sand the cut edges until they are smooth and even (photo B).

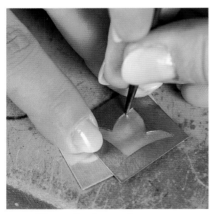

3 Place the base sheet on top of the metal sheet you wish to use for the inlay. Use a scribe to trace the shape of the negative space carefully and precisely onto the inlay metal.

4 Use the jeweler's saw to cut out the shape traced in step 3, making sure you follow the outside of the scribed lines. It is

better for the shape to be slightly large than too small.

5 Check whether the inlay shape fits into the negative space of the base piece. If the shape is too large, use a needle file or sandpaper to slowly remove metal on the edges where the shape does not fit. Keep checking the fit of the metal constantly. If the shape is too small, repeat steps 3–5 on a new piece of inlay metal.

6 Once the metal pieces fit together perfectly without gaps, place them on a flat soldering block (I prefer a fresh, honeycomb block) and flux around the seam where the two metals meet.

7 Solder the metals together with hard solder, letting the solder flow by means of capillary action. (I use stick solder when making a marriage of metal sheet.)

Add more solder if the initial amount used doesn't flow around the entire seam. Pickle and rinse the piece.

8 Use a file to remove any excess solder from the marriage of metal sheet. (This may be easier to accomplish if you slightly bend or dome the metal first.)

9 There are many options for using an inlay marriage of metal sheet. You can set it in a bezel as you would a stone, solder it onto other metalwork, or use it to create hollow forms; just be sure to use easy solder for all subsequent soldering and keep the heat of the torch away from the solder joints on the marriage of metal sheet.

Pattern Technique for Marriage of Metal

MATERIALS

Nonferrous sheet metals of your choice, each 22 gauge

TOOLS & SUPPLIES

Bench tool kit, page 27
Soldering kit, page 27

STEP BY STEP

1 Use the jeweler's saw to cut out the metal pieces you want to solder together. File or sand the cut edges to make all adjacent pieces perfectly flush.

2 Arrange the metal pieces on a flat honeycomb block to create the desired design.

3 Flux all seams to be soldered, and then use stick solder to join the metal pieces. Pickle and rinse the soldered metal.

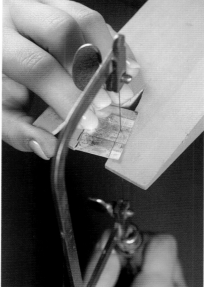

4 If desired, use the jeweler's saw to cut the marriage of metal sheet apart again, acting as if the metal is simply a new sheet. Using this method, you can achieve intricate designs without having to arrange small pieces. (Note: If you use this method to solder together two different colors of metal in strips, you can cut and arrange a checkerboard pattern, or you can cut the strips into more strips to create thinner metal lines.)

5 File the excess solder off the surface until all the joints are clean. Sand the metal with 220-grit paper, and then finish with 400-grit paper. A marriage of metal piece is most impressive with a matte finish. Use the finished sheet in any type of jewelry.

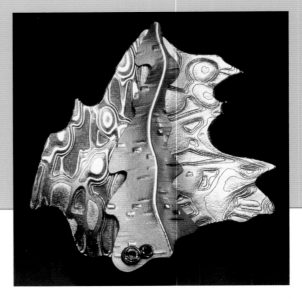

Mokume Gane

The mokume gane technique involves bonding layers of different colors of metal together, and then manipulating the layers to produce a pattern. This ancient Japanese technique, often abbreviated to mokume, gives metal a wood grain texture and appearance. Many people discuss making a mokume *billet*, or stack of bonded metals, by soldering individual layers together. This is not the accurate way to produce a billet for mokume. The correct method is to diffusion weld the layers together. In diffusion welding, the metal layers are heated in a kiln until the surface molecules of each layer bond without solder or any other intermediary metal binder. This process is extremely technical and requires a sizeable investment. Because it is now possible to purchase mokume laminate or sheet stock from metal suppliers, I have chosen to present three processes for patterning mokume without producing the billet.

Punch Patterning

This technique of punching the mokume to create its pattern is similar to chasing. You can use liner tools to chase intricate designs or simply make a series of indentions.

MATERIALS
Mokume sheet stock of your
choice, 14 or 18 gauge*
Sheet metal stock of your choice
for backing (optional)

TOOLS & SUPPLIES
Bench tool kit, page 27
Soldering kit, page 27
Grinding wheel attachment

*For the punch patterning method, the
mokume sheet stock should be 18
gauge. If you can only find 14-gauge
stock, you will need to use a rolling mill
to roll it down to 18 or even 20 gauge
before patterning. The sheet stock
should arrive annealed, but check with
your supplier prior to ordering. If you
start with 14-gauge sheet stock, you'll
probably need to anneal it halfway
through the rolling process.*

STEP BY STEP

1 Choose one side of the 18- or 20-gauge mokume sheet to be the top surface for your piece.

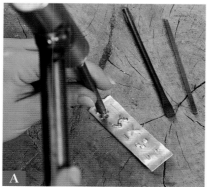

2 Punch the back side of the
metal sheet with the chasing
or repoussé tools of your choice,
placing the marks in an arrange-
ment that appeals to you (photo
A). Each tool will make a different
pattern on the mokume (photo B).
Do not punch the sheet farther
than halfway through its thickness. A punch that is too deep may
cause a hole in the metal when
the top of the raised surface is
sanded later. (Control the depth of
the punch by the force of the
hammer blow. It is best to err on
the side of making lighter hammer

strokes, as you can always add
subsequent punch marks to make
the pattern deeper.)

3 If punching has curved or
deformed the sheet, place
it on a steel block and use a rubber
or rawhide mallet to hammer it flat.

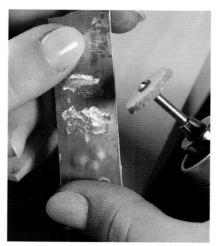

4 Grind or file off the raised
surfaces on the top side of
the punched metal. Once flattened, each punch mark should
expose several layers of metal, producing an intricate pattern.

5 To roll punch-patterned
metal thinner, first fill all
indentions on the back of the
sheet with solder (photo C). This
prevents any of the thinner areas
of the sheet from cracking or split-
ting. Anneal the sheet, and then
roll it through the rolling mill until

the desired thickness is achieved
(photo D). Alternatively, a solid
sheet of metal can be sweat soldered onto the back of the patterned mokume to make a
laminate. (This option is especially
helpful when the back of the
metal will show in the finished
piece.) Remember that rolling the
metal thinner will alter the
mokume pattern. Use this decorative metal in any jewelry project
you desire.

Gouge Patterning

MATERIALS

Mokume sheet stock of your choice, ⅛ or ¼ inch (3 or 6 mm) thick*

TOOLS & SUPPLIES

Assorted burrs and/or bull-nose chisel
Bench tool kit, page 27
Soldering kit, page 27

Using thicker sheet stock permits you to make more intricate gouge patterns.

STEP BY STEP

Figure 1

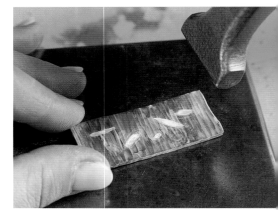

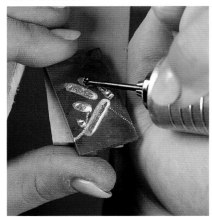

1 Use grinding burrs or a chisel to gouge patterns of your choice into the mokume sheet stock. Only gouge approximately one-third of the way through the thickness of the metal.

2 After gouging a simple pattern, round off the edges of each gouge using a grinding wheel attachment as shown in figure 1. (This prevents the edges of the gouges from turning over and creating air pockets when the sheet is forged.)

3 Place the gouged sheet stock on an anvil or large steel block, and use a forging hammer to flatten out the sheet. Hammer the higher surfaces first and concentrate the blows on the middle of the sheet. (It is easier to move the metal at the edges of the sheet. Therefore, to achieve a mokume sheet that is nice and even, you must hammer enough in the middle.) Anneal the metal sheet several times during this forging process.

4 Once the sheet is forged flat, gouge it some more. Gouge only one-third of the way through the thickness of the sheet. Repeat step 3 after this round of gouging.

5 After gouging and forging the sheet twice, anneal it. Make sure the metal surface is almost perfectly flat except for hammer marks. Roll the metal through the rolling mill until it reaches the desired thickness (see photo).

Twisted Wire Mokume

MATERIALS

Mokume sheet stock of your choice, 1/4 inch (6 mm) thick

TOOLS & SUPPLIES

Bench tool kit, page 27
Rolling mill with square groove
Vise
Soldering kit, page 27

STEP BY STEP

1 To make a wire, saw a length of mokume sheet stock that is approximately 5 mm wide. Make sure you cut the sheet straight and even. Roll the thin metal through a square groove on the rolling mill to make an even piece of square wire (see photo).

2 Secure the square wire in the vise. Hold the opposite end of the wire in a pair of pliers, and twist the metal (see photo). Twist it as tightly or as loosely as you like. With practice, you'll know what type of twist makes what type of mokume pattern.

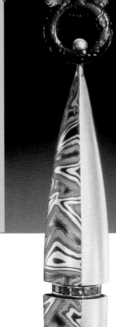

3 Open the rollers on the mill far apart so the edges of the twisted wire won't turn over and create air pockets. Slowly roll the twisted wire through a square groove on the rolling mill (see photo). Continue to roll the wire through the mill until it is completely square, and then anneal the wire.

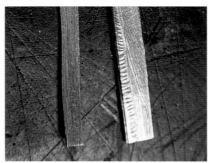

4 Roll the wire through the flat area of the rolling mill to make the metal more rectangular. Use the jeweler's saw to cut the metal in half, and the mokume pattern will be revealed on the inside. Once finished, use this surface of the metal for its decorative effect in any jewelry project.

Finishing Mokume

The finishing options for mokume gane depend on which metals are in the piece. A dark patina may only alter the appearance of one of the metals, producing an attractive contrast. Mokume can also be etched, making some layers higher than others (refer to pages 88–89 for further information on etching). Mokume looks best with a matte finish; a high polish conceals the different metal colors. For a nice clean look, scrub mokume with a green scrub pad or steel wool.

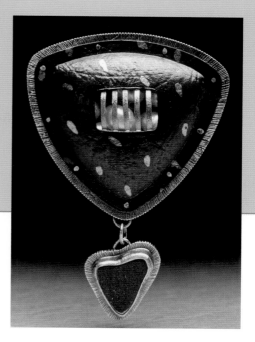

Solder Inlay

Solder inlay produces a subtle yet beautiful surface design on a piece of jewelry. A line drawing is made on a metal sheet with a jeweler's saw, a file, or a separating disc, and the negative space is inlayed with silver solder. Alternatively, metal can be roller printed and the recessed areas filled with solder to create a two-tone design.

MATERIALS
Sheet metal, 24 gauge, any type other than silver
Silver hard solder, stick form works best

TOOLS & SUPPLIES
Bench tool kit, page 27
Soldering kit, page 27

STEP BY STEP

1 Design a solder inlay pattern and draw or transfer it onto a small sheet of 24-gauge metal. (I recommend beginners use a sheet of metal that is no larger than 2 x 2 inches [5.1 x 5.1 cm]; a larger sheet of metal can warp from the heat.) The drawing can begin at the edge of the metal or farther away from the edge through a very small hole drilled with a 0.25-mm bit. Make sure the planned design does not cut the metal apart. If you are simply trying to solder two unconnected metal pieces, you won't be able to control the thickness of the solder line.

2 Saw the line drawing using a 1/0, 2/0, or 3/0 blade in the jeweler's saw. (Smaller blades make thinner lines.)

3 Place the metal on a flat honeycomb soldering block, and flux all the saw lines.

4 Heat the metal with the torch and run stick solder down all the sawn lines. Make sure the solder completely fills the lines.

5 Use a file to remove any excess solder from the inlay piece. (This may be easier to accomplish if you slightly bend or dome the metal first.)

6 There are many options for using a sheet with solder inlay. You can set it in a bezel as you would a stone, solder it onto other metalwork, or use it to create hollow forms; just be sure to use easy solder for all subsequent soldering and keep the heat of the torch away from the inlay.

Arched Earrings with Solder Inlay

Solder inlay is a straightforward way to combine metals that yields very handsome results. Although this earring design uses straight lines and hard angles, their random, informal placement implies casual sophistication.

MATERIALS

Copper sheet, 18 gauge
Sterling silver sheet, 24 gauge
Sterling silver ear posts and nuts

TOOLS & SUPPLIES

Soldering kit, page 27
Bench tool it, page 27
Large mandrel

STEP BY STEP

1 Measure and mark two rectangles on the 18-gauge copper sheet, each 1.5 x 2.8 cm. Use the jeweler's saw to cut out the rectangles, and then file their edges smooth.

2 Use a triangle needle file or a separating disc to carve a random pattern of straight grooves in each copper rectangle. (Refer to page 125, step 1 for further information on forming the lines for solder inlay.)

3 Apply flux to both copper rectangles, and then fill in their grooves with hard solder. Pickle and rinse the rectangles.

4 Using a rawhide mallet, gently bend the copper rectangles lengthwise around a large mandrel to give each piece a soft curve.

5 Use a bastard file to remove all excess solder from both rectangles, leaving the lines of solder inlay clean and clearly visible. Sand the pieces to a 220-grit finish.

6 Sand the bottom ends of each curved copper piece on a very low-grit piece of sandpaper. (This creates a flat joint on which to solder the bottom pieces of the earrings.)

7 Measure and mark two rectangles on the sterling silver sheet, each approximately 1.7 x 2.7 cm. Use the jeweler's saw to cut out these pieces.

8 Position one piece of inlayed copper to arch on top of one flat silver rectangle. (The silver base will slightly extend past the ends of the arch. Adjust this extra metal to be equal on both ends.)

Using the stick soldering method with medium solder, attach the copper arch to the silver base. Pickle and rinse the piece, and then repeat this step to join the second earring.

9 Use a jeweler's saw or a file to remove any excess sterling silver that extends past the arch.

File all edges with a bastard file. The joined elements should be flush and the seams clean.

10 On the back of each earring, measure and mark a centered point that is approximately 1 cm down from the top edge. Use easy solder to attach an ear post at the marked locations. Pickle and rinse the earrings.

11 Sand the earrings to a 400-grit finish, and give them a final matte finish with a green scrub pad.

Marriage of Metal Bracelet

A marriage of metal flower composed of sterling silver and nickel silver serves as a lovely focal point for this pearl bracelet and disguises its clasp.

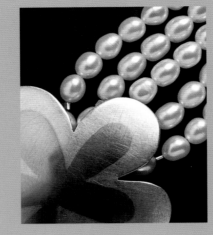

MATERIALS

Photocopied design templates, page 172
Sterling silver sheet, 24 gauge
Nickel silver sheet, 24 gauge
Sterling silver round wire, 16 gauge
Sterling silver round wire, 18 gauge
Tigertail wire
2 strands white freshwater pearls, approximately 4 mm
Silver French wire
Sterling silver crimp beads

TOOLS & SUPPLIES

Bench tool kit, page 27
Soldering kit, page 27

STEP BY STEP

1 Tape photocopied design template A to the 24-gauge sterling silver sheet. Use the jeweler's saw to cut out the outer contour of the flower. Pierce and saw out the interior flower. File all cut edges smooth.

2 Tape photocopied design template B to the 24-gauge nickel silver sheet. Use the jeweler's saw to cut out the small flower. File the cut edges smooth. Place the small nickel silver flower into the negative space in the sterling silver flower and make sure the fit is exact.

3 Following the instructions on page 118, step 7, solder these elements together with hard solder. Pickle and rinse the flower.

4 To make a back sheet for the marriage of metal, tape design template C to a piece of 24-gauge sterling silver sheet. Use the jeweler's saw to cut out the flower form.

5 Following the appliqué soldering method described on pages 96–97, appliqué the marriage of metal flower to the back sheet with easy solder. Pickle and rinse the piece.

6 Use the jeweler's saw to cut off any excess metal from the back sheet, making the sterling silver flower and the marriage of metal flower exactly the same size. File off any excess solder from the marriage of metal flower.

7 Place the marriage of metal flower face down in a low-dome dapping block, and gently dome the flower. File the marriage of metal side, and sand the piece to a 220-grit finish.

8 Saw a 1.7-cm length of the 16-gauge round sterling silver wire. Use round-nose pliers to form the wire into the shape shown in figure 1.

Figure 1

9 Using the pick-up solder method with easy solder, attach the shaped wire in the center of the back of the flower. Pickle and rinse the piece.

10 Use the 18-gauge round sterling silver wire to make a jump ring that is approximately 8 mm in diameter. Thread the jump ring onto the wire on the back of the flower. Use easy solder to close the jump ring around the wire. Pickle and rinse the piece.

11 Following the instructions on pages 156–157, make an S clasp using the 18-gauge sterling silver round wire.

12 Sand both sides of the flower to a 400-grit finish, making certain to remove all firescale.

13 String five strands of freshwater pearls, each 6 inches (15.2 cm) long. (Refer to the stringing directions on pages 162–163 as needed.) Use French wire and crimp beads to attach the one end of the five pearl strands to the 8-mm jump ring. Attach the opposite ends of the strands to the S clasp.

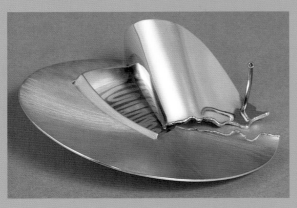

TOP LEFT: **Munya Avigail Upin**
Another Homage, 1980. 3.3 x 7 x 7 cm. Sterling silver, fine silver, copper; card woven, marriage of metal, fabricated, box clasp. Photo © artist

TOP RIGHT: **Jan Wehrens**
Untitled, 1979. 5.8 x 4.5 cm. 24-karat gold, 22-karat gold, silver, copper. Photo © George Meister. Collection of Die Neue Sammlung, Pinakothek der Moderne, Munich

CENTER LEFT: **Tedd R. McDonah**
Pendant, 1999. 10 x 3 x 4 cm. Sterling silver, copper, red jasper, antler; mokume gane, formed, fabricated. Photo © Alan McCoy

CENTER RIGHT: **Nicole Jacquard**
Gothic Interpretations, 1995. 19.5 x 13.5 x 8 cm. Silver, copper, 22-karat gold, thermoplastic, brass, patina; hand fabricated, etched, solder inlay. Photo © Kevin Montague

LEFT: **Debra Lynn Gold**
Nailed It, 1998. 5 x 13 x 13 cm. Sterling silver, nickel silver, silver solder, steel; forged, formed, fabricated, solder inlay, distressed finish, polished. Photo © artist

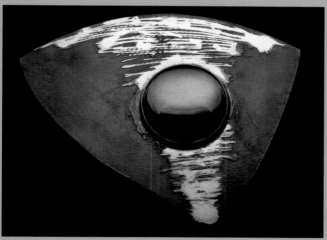

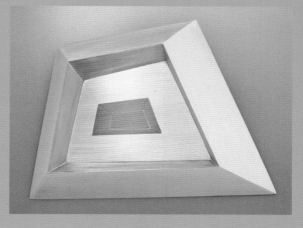

TOP LEFT: Hratch Babikian
Baguettes, 1990–1993. 5 cm tall. 14-karat yellow gold, sterling silver; carved, solder inlay, etched, polished, oxidized. Photo © artist

TOP CENTER: Brooke Battles
Women I've Known #5, 1998. 10 x 4 x 2 cm. Brass, sterling silver, 18-karat gold, fine silver, shell; hand fabricated, fused. Photo © Hap Sakwa

TOP RIGHT: Jane Garibaldi
Mokume Shield, 2002. 7 x 4 x 1 cm. Sterling silver, 14-karat gold, garnet; mokume gane, fabricated, formed, oxidized. Photo © Hap Sakwa

CENTER LEFT: Hratch Babikian
Tri Circle Onyx, 1990–1993. 5 x 5 cm. 14-karat yellow gold, sterling silver, onyx; fabricated, fused, carved, solder inlay, etched, set, oxidized. Photo © artist

CENTER RIGHT: Alexandra de Serpa Pimentel
Untitled, 1995. 4.9 x 4.9 x 0.6 cm. Sterling silver, patina; mokume gane, hand fabricated, soldered, riveted, whitened. Photo © artist

RIGHT: Cynthia Eid
Study in Depth, 1980. 2 x 3 x 0.5 cm. Silver, copper, brass, bronze; marriage of metal, constructed. Photo © artist

Adding Color

From setting gemstones to enameling, the techniques for introducing color into metal jewelry are some of the best loved and most exciting in the field. Use your new skills in two projects at the end of the chapter, on pages 142–145.

Torch-Fired Enameling

Torch firing enamels onto metal is an outstanding way to achieve interesting colors and textures on jewelry. This method is well suited for beginning enamelists who do not have or wish to buy a kiln and for jewelers working in a small shop. The following technique shows the most basic enamel application: sifting. With careful practice, however, almost any enameling technique can be torch fired.

MATERIALS
Flux enamel (if using transparent enamels)
Copper sheet or fine silver sheet, 20 gauge
Scouring powder or pumice
Enamel holding agent (binder)
Lead-free powered enamels of your choice

TOOLS & SUPPLIES
Bench tool kit, page 27
Small paintbrush
Screen enamel sifter
2 firebricks to support the mesh screen
Wire mesh screen, approximately 6 inches (15.2 cm) square, 18 to 16 gauge, ¼-inch (6 mm) holes
Safety glasses that protect from UV light, infrared light, and sodium flare (available from a glass blower's or welder's supply store)
Soldering kit, page 27
Enameling trivet to fit piece

Enameling screen, trivets, sifters, powdered enamel

Note: These instructions are for using opaque enamels. If you wish to use transparent enamels, you must first apply a base coat of flux enamel to the metal.

STEP BY STEP
Preparing the Metal

1 Use the jeweler's saw to cut the copper or fine silver sheet into a shape to enamel. File the cut edges smooth, and then clean the metal with scouring powder or pumice. (Do not clean the metal with steel wool, because any leftover steel particles could have negative reactions with the enamels.) Make sure the water sheets off the metal and does not bead up. Hold the clean metal by its edges to avoid fingerprints.

RIGHT: **Liz Mathews**
Locket, 2003. 7.6 x 3.8 cm.
Silver, enamel, copper, ribbon,
crayon; hand fabricated, die
formed. Photo © Norman Watkins

FAR RIGHT: **Caroline Gore**
Fin 2, 2003. 7.5 x 7.5 x 2.5 cm.
24-karat gold, copper, sterling
silver, enamel. Photo © artist

Applying & Firing a Base Coat

2 Use a small brush to paint a thin, even coat of holding agent onto the front surface of the metal form. This fixative helps the dry enamel stick to the metal surface.

3 While the holding agent is wet, use a screen enamel sifter to gently sift an even layer of dry enamel onto the metal and coat the surface completely.

4 Arrange the firebricks on the soldering area so the mesh screen rests on top of the bricks. Because the piece will be heated from below, there should be enough space under the screen to accommodate the torch. Place the enamel-covered metal directly on the mesh screen (see photo). Let the holding agent dry completely.

5 Light the torch and open the gas to form a large, bushy flame. The flame should be hot, but not roaring. (When torch firing enamel, a flame that is too large produces heat that can be difficult to control.) Direct the flame under the wire mesh screen and carefully rotate the flame around the whole piece. Gently heat the piece until the enamel completely fuses and looks glassy and smooth. Remove the heat and let the piece air cool.

Applying & Firing a Counter Enamel

6 Clean the back of the metal to remove all oxidation caused by the initial firing. Repeat steps 2 and 3 to sift a new layer of enamel onto the back of the metal. (Coating the back, a process known as counter enameling, prevents the enamel on the front from chipping or flaking off. If enamel were fired only on the front of a piece, the metal would be under uneven surface stress.) Choose a color for the back if you like, or simply use clear flux enamel. (Coloring the back can be an interesting design choice, especially if you plan to set the enamel and then pierce a sheet through which the color will show.)

7 Place the metal on an appropriately sized trivet. Make sure the metal edges are resting on the trivet and that no part of the front surface of the enamel will be marred by the trivet. Repeat step 5 to fire the counter enamel. The metal now has a base coat on the front and a counter enamel on the back.

Creating the Design

8 Continue to add layers of enamel as desired to achieve different colors or surface treatments. Experiment to see how the torch flame affects the enamels and the colors being used. Each color reacts differently to the heat, and overheating some colors can generate interesting results. Note that warm colors such as orange and yellow tend to burn out quickly. Overheating them can produce black spots or edges on a piece. Cooler colors such as green and blue work well with torch firing. Opaque colors furnish different results than transparent colors. I suggest experimenting with different types of enamel colors and heat levels to discover all the interesting ways in which the enamel reacts.

Enamel Textures

One creative way to use the enameling process is to vary the surface appearance and texture of the enamel. Enamel fuses to metal in three phases. In the first fusing stage, the enamel becomes crystal-like in appearance and takes on what is known as a sugar-coat texture. In the next stage, the enamel fuses to the metal a little more and looks like the skin of an orange. This is known as an orange-peel texture. Finally, in the third stage, the enamel fully fuses into a glossy surface and a completely smooth texture. You can torch fire enamel to any of these stages, depending on the surface texture that pleases you. If you plan to create a sugar-coat or an orange-peel texture, you must first fire a flux enamel base coat onto the metal. This base coat gives the second layer, the one you wish to have a sugar-coat or an orange-peel texture, something to fuse to. If there is no base coat under the colored enamel, chances are high that the enamel will quickly flake off the metal, because it will not have had a chance to fuse to the metal completely.

Other Enameling Techniques

There are numerous ways to use enamel in jewelry, and with new technologies, the application methods and creative possibilities continue to grow. Here is a glossary of the most widely practiced techniques. If this introduction to enameling has stirred your interest, I encourage you to seek out books and workshops devoted to the topic.

Cloisonné

This is a French term meaning "cell." In this technique, small, thin wires are used to make *cloisons* (cells), which are then attached to a sheet of metal and filled with different enamel colors.

Champlevé

In champlevé, French for "raised field," enamel fills recessed areas on a metal surface. To create the depressions, the metal is etched, or a pierced metal sheet is soldered onto a solid base sheet. The upper metal level remains exposed after the enamel is added.

Basse Taille

In this technique, a pattern is created on a metal sheet by means of milling, engraving, chasing, or stamping. Transparent enamels are applied to the metal, and the pattern shows through the enamel when fired.

ABOVE: **Michelle Ritter**
Labyrinth Rings, 2003. Each, 5 x 6 x 6 cm. Wood, aluminum, silver, resin, citrine, garnet, peridot; turned, fabricated, textured, molded, inlay. Photo © Helen Shirk

RIGHT: **Sadie Shu Ping Wang**
Star Circle Brooch, 2003. 7.6 x 6.4 x 1 cm. Sterling silver, resin; fabricated. Photo © Azad Photo

Grisaille

Grisaille is a technique that yields a black-and-white enamel. Fired black enamel is used as a background, and white enamel is slowly painted and fired in layers on top of the black to create an image.

Limoges

Though similar to cloisonné, Limoges differs in that no wires are used to separate the colors. The finished, freehand image is often very painterly in appearance.

Plique-Á-Jour

Plique-á-jour is a French term meaning "membrane through which passes the light of day." This style of enamel work looks similar to stained glass. Wires are fabricated into a structure of cells, and each cell is filled with transparent enamel. The cells may also be created by piercing sheet metal and by etching completely through sheet metal.

Stenciling

In this process, enamel is sifted over a stencil made of thick paper or Mylar. The stencil's cutout design is transferred in enamel to the metal surface. Similarly, enamel may be applied to metal through a silkscreen in the same manner ink is applied to cloth.

Resin Inlay

Resin inlay is a quick and creative way to add color to jewelry. A two-part epoxy resin is mixed, colored with pigments, and then poured into a recessed area in a metal surface. There are several commercial resins on the market. If you choose to use a commercial resin, simply follow the manufacturer's instructions.

MATERIALS
Sheet metal of your choice, 18 to 24 gauge
Two-part epoxy resin (not the quick-drying variety) or commercial resin
Airbrush or other water-based pigments

TOOLS & SUPPLIES
Bench tool kit, page 27
Soldering kit, page 27
Toothpicks
Wax file (optional)
Sandpaper, 600 grit
Polishing cloth (optional)
Toothbrush, if needed
Soap, if needed

STEP BY STEP

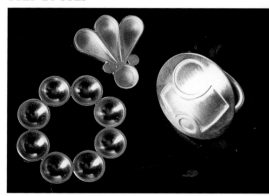

1 Using the sheet metal, fabricate a piece of jewelry with one or more recessed surface areas, or cells, to hold the liquid epoxy resin (see photo for examples). The cells can be made in any number of ways. An open, shallow box shape works well, as does a layer of pierced metal soldered onto a solid metal sheet. Burred areas or the concave sections of domed areas can be filled with resin. Wires can be appliquéd to sheet metal, creating a faux cloisonné. The only requirement is that the cells you create must have sides (barriers) to contain the resin while it is in its liquid state.

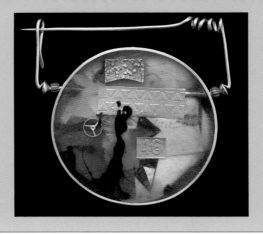

FAR LEFT: **Brian Meek**
Hidden Hazards 2A: Saxon Violence,
2005. 7 x 1 cm. Sterling silver, resin
enamel. Photo © artist

LEFT: **Jacqueline Myers**
Pin/Reversible Fibula (Side 2), 1994.
7 x 5.7 x 0.6 cm. Sterling silver beads,
resin mixed with powder paint pigments,
gold foil, found objects; hand fabricated,
etched. Photo © D. James Dee

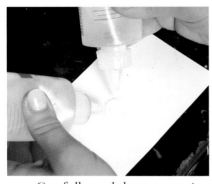

2 Carefully read the epoxy resin manufacturer's safety precautions and directions for use. Mix the two-part epoxy resin as instructed, estimating the amount of resin needed to fill the recessed area. (If several areas are to be filled, you may want to mix several batches of resin because it may begin to set before all areas can be filled.)

stir the resin and the pigment together (photo B) until it is thoroughly mixed and uniform in color. Do not stir too quickly or bubbles will form in the resin.

5 Quickly and lightly pass a soldering torch over the resin to get rid of any air bubbles. Do not let the resin get too hot or it will begin to burn and will not set correctly, or the color may change.

A

3 Add one or two drops of the pigment to the mixed resin (photo A). Do not add too much pigment or it will interfere with the chemical reaction that causes the resin to set. Slowly but steadily

4 Pour or use a toothpick to transfer the resin into the cells of the jewelry piece until they are full.

6 Set aside the resin-filled jewelry piece, letting it harden overnight. Once the resin is completely set, use a bastard file or a wax file to remove any overflow (see photo).

7 Sand the resin to a 600-grit, matte finish. If you desire a shinier finish, rub the piece on a polishing cloth. If this leaves black streaks on the inlay, gently scrub the piece with a toothbrush and some soap to remove them.

BENCH TIP

Let your imagination go wild, and experiment with placing found objects in resin inlays. For example, place a picture in a metal "frame" and cover it with clear resin. Include seeds, pearls, grass, sand—all sorts of things can create texture, pattern, and meaning.

Flush Stone Setting

You can use a flush setting to secure small (0.5 to 3.5 mm), round brilliant-cut stones. The term *flush* means that the table of the stone is flush with the surface of the metal, while the girdle of the stone actually sits beneath the surface. A small amount of metal is pushed over the girdle to hold the stone firmly in place.

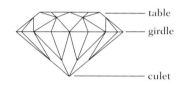

table — girdle — culet

MATERIALS

Round brilliant-cut stones,
0.5 to 3.5 mm in diameter
Metal of your choice, at least
0.75 mm thicker in width than
the distance from the table to
the girdle of the stone

TOOLS & SUPPLIES

Digital calipers
Bench tool kit, page 27
90-degree hart burrs, approximately 0.1 mm smaller than
the size of the stones
Setting tool

New Tool *A setting tool is used to push metal over a flush-set, round-cut stone. Concurrently, this tool acts as a burnisher. It makes the area around the set stone bright due to the force exerted on the metal when the stone is set. This tool looks similar to a center punch, but it has a smooth round end instead of a sharp pointed end.*

Assorted cabochons and faceted stones, pearl beads

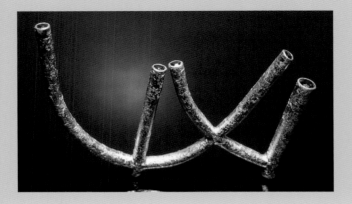

STEP BY STEP

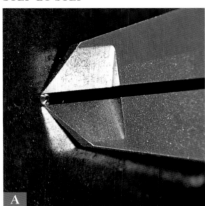

1 Use digital calipers to measure the size of the stone to be set (photo A). Determine and mark a location for the setting on the metal. Drill a hole at the marked point that is smaller than the diameter of the stone (photo B). (Although there is no hard and fast rule for the size of this hole, I suggest making it at least 0.75 mm smaller than the diameter of the stone.)

Figure 1

2 Select a 90-degree hart burr (see example, figure 1) that is approximately 0.1 mm smaller than the stone to be set. Using the correct size burr is essential for flush setting stones. It is better to use a burr that is too small than one that is too large. (After using a smaller burr, you can slowly grind out the area that needs to be larger. You cannot, however, always find a larger stone to fit a hole that has been burred too large.)

3 Insert the burr into the flexible shaft. Where the hole was drilled in step 1, slowly begin to make a seat for the stone in the metal. Cut out the seat until the girdle of the burr is just below the surface of the metal. (You can

mentally equate the girdle of the bur with the girdle of the stone.) Dip the burr into beeswax or oil as needed for easier cutting.

4 Place the stone to be set in the hole burred out in step 3. The stone should make a slight "snap" when it fits into the hole.

5 Use the setting tool to push the edge of the metal over and around the stone. Make firm, circular motions with the setting tool as you work around the edge of the stone. Repeat this several times in both directions until the stone is secure.

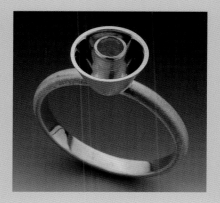

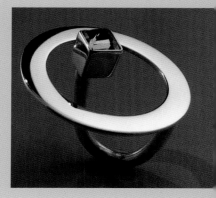

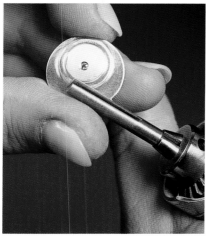

6 Test the stone to verify that it is firmly set. To do this, place any type of attachment in the flexible shaft. As it rotates, hold the shaft of the attachment against the metal to make a slight vibration. If the stone begins to move, it is not set tightly enough. If it stays in place, chances are you've made a secure setting.

A small amount of metal pushed over the girdle holds the stone in place.

Bezel Stone Setting

A bezel is a thin strip of metal that surrounds a stone to keep it firmly in place. Bezels can be made in any shape to fit around any stone. This includes irregular free-form stones, as well as oval, round, square, emerald-cut, or marquis ones. Bezels can be used for cabochons as well as for faceted stones.

New Tools *A bezel rocker and a bezel pusher are two hand tools made for pushing over a bezel setting to hold a stone in place. Some jewelers prefer using a bezel pusher, which has a square head, rather than a bezel rocker, which has a rectangular curved head. Choose the tool based on personal preference.*

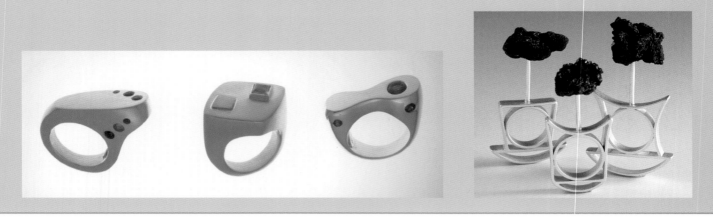

Making a Simple Bezel for a Round Cabochon

MATERIALS

Bezel wire or sheet metal strip,
  24 to 26 gauge
Cabochon of your choice
Sheet metal, any type or gauge, or
  jewelry piece of your choice

TOOLS & SUPPLIES

Bench tool kit, page 27
Soldering kit, page 27
Bezel rocker or pusher

STEP BY STEP

Figure 1   *Figure 2*   *Figure 3*

1 Wrap the bezel wire or metal strip around the base of the cabochon to determine the proper length of the metal. Mark the metal where the strip crosses its end (see photo), and cut the metal at this point with the jeweler's saw. The bezel should be tall enough to cover the start of the curvature of the cabochon. (Figure 1 shows a bezel that is too tall. Figure 2 shows a bezel that is too short. Figure 3 shows a bezel that is the correct height.)

2 Position the two ends of the bezel strip to fit together perfectly. Using one small paillon of hard solder and a solder pick, solder the ends together. Pickle and rinse the metal, clean up any extra solder from the joint, and sand the bezel to a 400-grit finish.

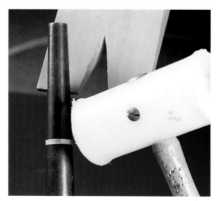

3 Place the bezel on a small mandrel, and lightly hammer it with a wooden or rawhide mallet to make it completely round. Sand the bottom of the bezel flat.

4 Check the size of the bezel against the size of the stone to be set. The stone should fit in the bezel from the top without being forced, and there should be a little room for movement. Too much room, however, is not good. The stone shouldn't be able to slide back and forth within the framework of the bezel.

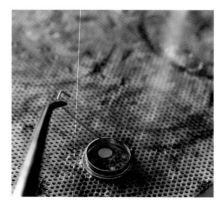

5 Carefully solder the bezel onto the sheet metal or jewelry piece of your choice. Make sure the solder joint on the bezel does not come unsoldered when the bezel is attached. Pickle and rinse the metal.

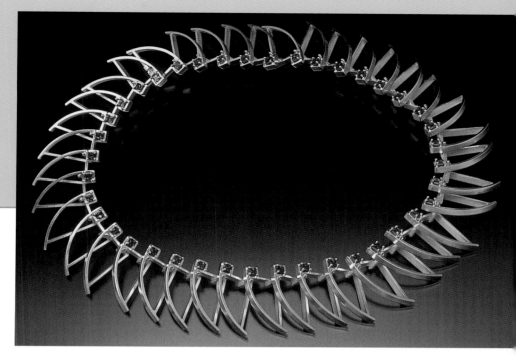

6 Finish fabricating the jewelry piece completely. No soldering or other type of finishing work should have to be done after the stone is set unless it is a cold technique that does not involve chemicals or abrasives. Setting the stone should always be the last step.

7 Place the stone in the bezel. Starting with the bezel rocker or pusher at the 12 o'clock position, begin gently pushing a small amount of metal over the stone. Next, push over a small amount of metal at the 6 o'clock position, then at 3 o'clock, and finally at 9 o'clock. This ensures that the stone is evenly held in place and prevents the bezel from crimping. (If you are setting a large stone, you may wish to repeat the process at 2 o'clock, 7 o'clock, and so on.)

8 Use the bezel rocker to push the remaining bezel metal over the stone.

9 Use the burnisher to make the bezel evenly snug around the stone. Rub the metal in smooth strokes. This burnishing will slightly polish the bezel. If you do not desire a shiny bezel, gently and carefully finish it as you wish, making sure you don't touch the cabochon with the finishing agent.

Orange Sapphire Ring

Three faceted, flush-set stones elevate a simple band into a work of exquisite beauty. Use this project to develop your stone-setting skills, and then make it your own by varying the stone size, color, and placement.

MATERIALS

Sterling silver square wire,
2 x 2 mm
Sterling silver rectangular wire,
2 x 8 mm
3 orange, round, faceted sapphires
(or stone of your choice), each
1.5 mm in diameter

TOOLS & SUPPLIES

Bench tool kit, page 27
Soldering kit, page 27
Ring mandrel
Separators
90-degree hart burr, approximately
0.1 mm smaller than the size of
the stones
Setting tool

STEP BY STEP

1 Following the chart on page 172, determine the length of metal required for your ring size. Measure and mark this length on the 2 x 2-mm sterling silver square wire, and use the jeweler's saw to cut the wire to this length.

2 File the ends of the cut wire flush. Bring together the ends of the wire to make a band, and solder it closed with hard solder. Pickle and rinse the band.

3 Place the sterling silver band on the ring mandrel, and hammer it with a rawhide mallet to make it round.

4 File and sand the solder joint on the silver band.

5 Measure and mark a 1.5-cm length of the 2 x 8-mm sterling silver rectangular wire. Use the jeweler's saw to cut the wire to this length, and file the ends smooth and flush.

6 Use a large mandrel and a rawhide mallet to bend the rectangular wire gently, giving it a soft curve.

7 Open the separators to 7.5 mm, and mark the center point of the silver rectangular wire. Make one centered mark on each side of the center point that is 4 mm away from it.

8 Draw a centerline down the length of the silver rectangular wire. (You will use this line to center the stones on the top of the ring.)

9 Dimple each of the three marks made in step 7, and then drill a 1-mm hole at each location.

10 Align the solder joint of the band underneath the curved and drilled silver rectangular wire, and secure the band in place with cross-locking tweezers. Use easy solder to attach the band to the center of the silver rectangular wire. Pickle and rinse the ring.

11 Following the instructions on pages 137–139, flush set each stone into the ring.

12 Give the ring the final finish of your choice. (I used heavy-grit steel wool to create a partially shiny finish.)

Cuttlefish-Cast Tie Tack

Cast a sophisticated tie tack or lapel pin from recycled scraps of gold. One particularly clever design feature is that the setting for the sapphire is carved directly into the cuttlefish.

MATERIALS
Dried cuttlefish
Scrap metal, 18-karat gold
Round wire, 18-karat gold, 18 gauge
Solder for 18-karat gold, medium and easy
Commercial tie-tack pin and nut
Round, faceted blue sapphire or stone of your choice, 1.5 mm in diameter

TOOLS & SUPPLIES
Bench tool kit, page 27
Carving tools, such as a craft knife, burrs, a scribe, or a plastic knife
90-degree hart burr, approximately 0.1 mm smaller than the size of the stone
Binding wire
Ceramic crucible with tongs
Boric acid
Soldering kit, page 27
Setting tool

STEP BY STEP

1 Following steps 1–3 on page 78, prepare the dried cuttlefish for casting.

2 Use a carving tool to carve a 10 x 8-mm rectangle into one side of the cuttlefish that is approximately 2 mm deep. Use a round burr to hand carve a round depression in one corner of the rectangle. (This depression will be the setting for the stone.)

3 Place the sides of the cuttlefish together, and carve a sprue channel from the top, right side of the carved rectangle to the top end of the cuttlefish. Enlarge the sprue channel opening at the top of the cuttlefish. Secure the cuttlefish halves with binding wire.

4 Melt and cast the gold scrap as described in steps 7 and 8 on page 79.

5 Let the cuttlefish and the cast metal cool, and then open the mold. Remove the cast gold rectangle from the cuttlefish, and pickle and rinse the cast metal.

6 Use a barrette needle file to flatten the top of the depression for the stone.

7 Measure the length of the top and the right side of the cast gold rectangle and add 2 mm to these measurements. Use the jeweler's saw to cut two small pieces of the round, 18-karat gold wire to these measurements. Sand the ends of the cut wires flat.

8 Position the top wire above the casting so that 1 mm of wire extends past each end. Position the wire on the right side of the casting so one end touches the top wire. Use 18-karat gold medium solder to attach the gold wires in place. Pickle and rinse the piece.

9 Sand the overhanging wire ends so they are slightly round and will not catch on clothing.

10 Use 18-karat gold easy solder to attach the commercial tie-tack pin to the center of the back of the piece. Pickle and rinse the piece.

11 With the setting tool, flush set the 1.5-mm blue sapphire in the depression on the tie tack (refer to steps 4–6 on pages 138 and 139).

12 Polish the tie tack to a rouge finish with the polishing machine or a flexible shaft polishing attachment.

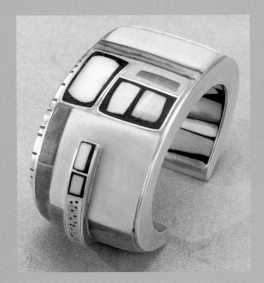

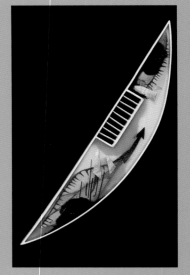

TOP LEFT: **Nancy Daniels-Hubert**
mmHMHmm, 2003. 5.7 x 19.7 cm. Sterling silver, fossilized wooly mammoth ivory, resin; fabricated, cut, inlay, finished. Photo © Jerry Anthony

TOP RIGHT: **Natalya Pinchuk**
Doodles Necklace, 2004. 4 x 20 x 20 cm. Copper, enamel, sterling silver, 22-karat gold, stainless steel; electroformed. Photo © artist

CENTER LEFT: **K.C. Calum**
Untitled, 2004. 18 x 18 x 0.5 cm. Sterling silver, epoxy resin; inlay. Photo © artist

CENTER MIDDLE: **Anne Goddard**
Serenity Wheel, 2003. 6.2 x 3 x 2 cm. Sterling silver, fine silver, enamel, peridot, 14-karat gold; basse taille, hand stamped, hand fabricated, riveted, tube bezel. Photo © Robert Diamante

CENTER RIGHT: **Jacqueline Myers**
Pin/Windows, 2000. 2.5 x 14 x 0.6 cm. Sterling silver, resin mixed with powder paint pigments, gold foil, found objects; hand fabricated, etched. Photo © D. James Dee

BOTTOM LEFT: **Jeffrey Clancy**
Neck Composition with Cube (detail), 2002. 50 x 31 x 31 cm. Copper, enamel, silver, latex, patina; electroformed, hand fabricated, oxidized. Photo © Helen Shirk

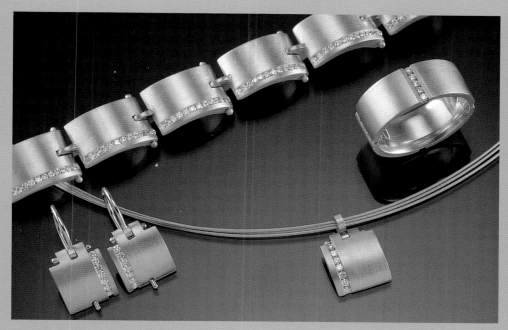

TOP LEFT: Lee Angelo Marraccini
Wide Apostrophe Collection, 2003. Pendant, 1 x 1 x 0.3 cm. 18-karat yellow gold, 18-karat white gold, diamonds; cast, fabricated, assembled, balled-wire riveted, channel set, pressure-fit closure. Photo © Pam Perugi Marraccini

TOP RIGHT: Beth Rosengard
Branch, 2001. 5.7 x 3.8 x 0.6 cm. 14-karat gold, 18-karat gold, 22-karat gold, sterling silver, coral, carnelian agate, amethyst, citrine, chrome diopside; bezel and prong settings, fabricated. Photo © artist

CENTER LEFT: Rob Jackson
Diamond Solitaire, 2004. 2.6 x 2.2 x 0.7 cm. Wrought-iron nail, 22-karat gold, diamond; hand fabricated, tension set. Photo © artist

CENTER MIDDLE: Ilana Rabinovich-Slonim
Completeness, 2003. 2 x 2.4 x 2.4 cm. Sterling silver, polyester; hand fabricated, silver slivers cast in polyester. Photo © Eli Mazor

CENTER RIGHT: Dianne M. Reilly
Venus, 2004. 2.5 x 5.1 cm. Enamel, fine silver, gold; hand fabricated, constructed, set. Photo © artist

BOTTOM RIGHT: Karen L. Cohen
Paisley Pleasures, 2002. 5.7 x 5.7 x 1 cm. Leaded enamels, fine silver, 22-karat gold, sterling silver, freshwater pearls, fine silver foil, gold foil, liquid gold; cloisonné, domed, hand fabricated, soldered, fused, engraved, alloyed, drawn, overglazed. Photo © Ralph Gabriner

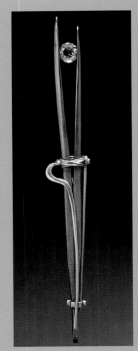

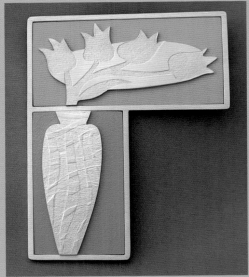

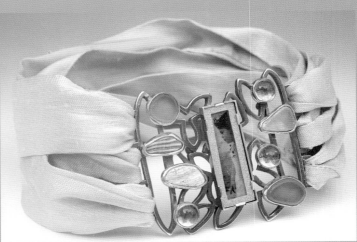

TOP LEFT: **Natasha Wozniak**
Wish-Fulfilling Vine Earrings, 2004. Each, 6 x 3 x 0.5 cm. 18-karat gold, green tourmalines; repoussé, forged, hand fabricated. Photo © Ralph Gabriner

TOP CENTER: **Patricia McAleer**
Red Leafy Sea Dragon Pendant, 2001. 16.1 x 8.9 x 1.9 cm. 14-karat yellow gold, fine silver, sterling silver, agate, pearl, moonstone, enamel; hollow core cast, corrugated, hand fabricated. Photo © Robert Sanders

TOP RIGHT: **Andy Cooperman**
Forceps, 1998. 7.6 cm long. Shibuishi, 14-karat gold, 18-karat gold, diamond; riveted, fabricated, forged. Photo © Doug Yaple

CENTER LEFT: **Jackie Anderson**
Spring Brooch, 2005. 6.7 x 5.3 x 0.7 cm. Sterling silver, wood laminate; roller printed, hand fabricated. Photo © artist

CENTER RIGHT: **Loretta Fontaine**
Eva on the Beach Bracelet/Necklace, 2004. 7.4 x 7.4 x 3.4 cm. 22-karat gold, sterling silver, color photograph, mica, aquamarine, sea glass, barnacle, dupioni silk, patina; hand fabricated, granulation, bezel set, tab set, sewn. Photo © artist. Courtesy of Taboo Studio, San Diego, California

BOTTOM LEFT: **Hratch Babikian**
Commitment Rings, 2004. Each, 2 x 2 cm. 18-karat red gold, diamonds; carved, formed, set. Photo © artist

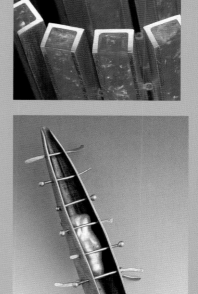

TOP LEFT: **Kathleen Browne**
Lucky, 2005. 9.2 x 9.2 x 1.3 cm. Fine silver, sterling silver, enamel, decals; die formed, fabricated, oxidized, hand printed. Photos © artist

TOP RIGHT: **Dayna Mae Orione**
Fire and Ice, 2002. 7.6 x 22.9 x 0.6 cm. Silver, resin, glass, carnelian; hinged, hand fabricated. Photos © Alan Farkas

CENTER LEFT: **Beate Eismann**
necklace, 2002. 47 cm long. Copper, German silver, enamel; sawed, riveted.
Photo © Helga Schulze-Brinkop

BOTTOM RIGHT: **Brooke Battles**
Pod Brooch, 1997. 10 x 1 x 1 cm. Sterling silver, 14-karat gold, pearl; fabricated, oxidized. Photo © John Werner

Mechanisms

A well-designed and well-executed mechanism not only functions impeccably but can also be a breathtaking work of art. The components that link elements and make jewelry wearable should be given just as much thought, and be created with just as much care, as any piece you undertake. At the end of this chapter, on page 164, is a project that incorporates a handmade pin stem and catch.

Findings

Certain components simply ease the jewelry fabrication process, while others are required to make finished pieces wearable. These elements are called findings. Those that make a piece wearable include bails, clasps, pin backs, ear wires, ear posts, and nuts. Those that ease construction include jump rings, settings, bezels, crimp beads, head pins, and eye pins. Jewelry supply stores and catalogs sell an incredible variety of mass-produced findings for those who do not wish to make their own.

Jump Rings

One of the most common and useful jewelry findings is the jump ring. Made from any shape or size of wire, a jump ring is used to connect parts, or it can stand alone as a complete ring. It is important to know how to form a jump ring correctly and open and close one properly.

MATERIALS
Wire, metal and gauge of your choice

TOOLS & SUPPLIES
Mandrel, diameter equal to desired jump ring size
Bench tool kit, page 27
Soldering kit, page 27 (optional)

From left: assorted jump rings, end caps, head pins, crimp beads, single-cup bead tips

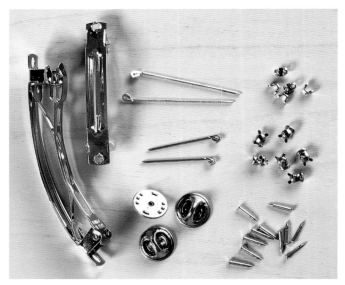

Commercial barrette, brooch, and pin findings, including pin stems, catches, joints, scatter pin posts, clasps

STEP BY STEP

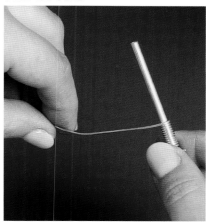

1 Neatly wrap the wire around the mandrel, making sure each revolution touches the previous revolution.

2 If you're making a lot of jump rings, then make a long coil. A long coil of heavy-gauge wire is easy to saw apart. However, if you're using a thin wire gauge and making small jump rings, use snips to cut the long coil into sections that are approximately 1 inch (2.5 cm) long. Smaller sections of coiled thin wire are easier to saw apart.

3 Firmly hold the coil of wire in your fingers and rest it on the bench pin.

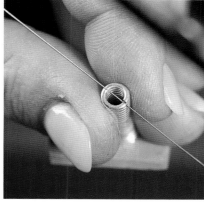

4 Beginning at the top of the coil, use the jeweler's saw to cut the rings apart. Hold the saw blade perpendicular to the wire and cut the rings at a 90-degree angle.

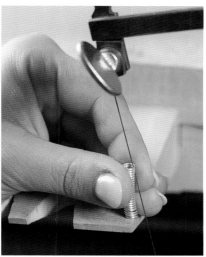

5 Saw all the way down the length of the coil at a slight angle, making sure you hold the coil tightly in your fingers.

6 To open and close a jump ring, hold each side of the cut with a pair of pliers. (I use chain-nose pliers on one side and flat-nose pliers on the other.) Move the ends of the ring side to side on the same plane rather than in and out like a lobster claw.

7 After using a jump ring to connect parts or as a decorative element, I recommend soldering its ends closed. Jump rings made of thin-gauge wire can stretch under tension and come apart unless they are soldered. When soldering jump rings made from thick wire, always sand the cut ends before joining them to create a smooth-looking ring.

Earring Findings

There are two main types of earring findings: those for pierced ears and those that that clip onto the ear.

Pierced Earring Findings: Ear Posts, Ear Nuts & French Wires

The post is a hard, straight wire that passes through the earlobe. Several varieties of posts are commercially available, or you can make your own. (I find it unnecessary to make earring posts by hand.) Posts are manufactured in several lengths and come with round pads of different diameters for ease in soldering. If you are a beginning jeweler and are having difficulty soldering on small wires, you may want to use commercial earring posts that have a 1.5-mm pad on one end. This pad will prevent you from melting the end of the post when soldering it to the back of an earring.

A nut secures a post earring to the ear, and there are many different nut sizes and designs. Always select a nut with a hole that fits the size of the ear post you're using.

Commercial earring findings for pierced and non-pierced ears, including ear wires, ear nuts, posts, paddles, hinges, ear screws

When a pierced earring is designed to dangle from the earlobe rather than sit directly on it, French wires are a great option. It is quite simple to make your own French wires, and you can show a great deal of creativity in constructing them by altering their shape or the length of the tail that passes through the ear. Jewelry and beading suppliers offer a large selection of commercial French wires if you wish to purchase them premade.

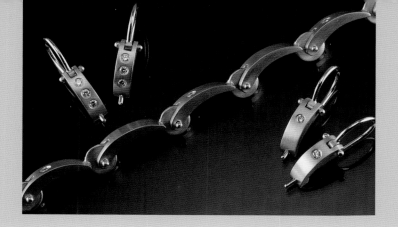

Soldering an Ear Post

Once you have created a pair of earrings, the last soldering step is attaching the posts. You must carefully place the posts so the earrings will hang correctly on the ear, and it will take practice to attach posts in the right place. If you have made a pair of small studs that are approximately 5 mm in diameter, it is safe to place the posts in the middle of the earrings. It is reasonably safe to attach posts near the top of larger earrings, but the placement will vary.

MATERIALS
Finished earrings
Ear posts

TOOLS & SUPPLIES
Soldering kit, page 27

STEP BY STEP

1 Flux the back of one earring. Cut some solder paillons and place them on a spare charcoal block.

2 Use a pair of cross-locking tweezers to pick up one ear post, with the end to be soldered farthest away from the tweezer tips. Dip the end to be soldered into the flux (see photo).

3 Light the torch and adjust the gas to create a medium-hot flame. Pick up a paillon of solder directly with the ear post. Use the torch to melt the solder onto the end of the post.

4 Heat the back of the earring with the flame until the flux looks glassy. While still holding the post in the cross-locking tweezers, place it into position, and continue to heat the earring (see photo). To keep from melting the ear post, direct most of the heat onto the earring, not the post. Heat the joint until the solder from the ear post flows and the ear post is secure. Pickle and rinse the earring.

5 Repeat steps 1–4 to solder a post onto the second earring.

Clip-On Earring Findings

The most common type of clip-on earring finding has a paddle and a hinge and is easy to attach. The hinge is soldered onto the earring in a low position so that when the paddle is attached to the hinge it rests on the upper part of the earring. The placement of the hinge and the paddle must be well thought out so that the earring will hang nicely on the ear.

LEFT: **Nichole Bowes**
Woven Chain, 2004. 20 x 15 x 1.5 cm.
Sterling silver, fine silver, garnets; hand fabricated, riveted, tube set, woven. Photo © artist

RIGHT: **Marguerite Chiang Manteau**
Broken Chain Necklace, 2004. 40.6 x 20.3 cm. Fine silver, 18-karat gold; hand fabricated, file finished. Photo © Hap Sakwa

FAR RIGHT: **Junghyun Woo**
Untitled, 1999. Each, 18 cm long. Sterling silver; hand fabricated. Photo © Munch Studio

Finishing Raw Snake Chain

One popular type of commercial chain is the snake chain. Its beauty lies in its simplicity and ability to complement many different styles of pendants. By knowing how to finish raw snake chain, you can save money and make a chain in any length you wish.

MATERIALS

Tubing to snugly fit the outside diameter (OD) of the snake chain
Round wire jump rings, 18 gauge, 3 to 4 mm in diameter
Unfinished commercial snake chain

TOOLS & SUPPLIES

Bench tool kit, page 27
Soldering kit, page 27

STEP BY STEP

1 Use the jeweler's saw to cut two 3- to 4-mm lengths of tubing. File and sand the cut tubing ends until they are flat and smooth.

Chains

Chains play diverse roles. They can stand alone as a lovely necklace, contribute to a larger jewelry design, or act solely to support a pendant. There is an infinite variety of chain patterns to make by hand or to purchase, such as curb, link, bead, and herringbone chain.

Assorted handmade chains

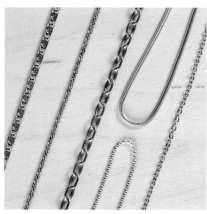

Assorted commercial chains

2 Place the tubing on the soldering block, and position one jump ring next to each piece of tubing so the curve of the jump ring sits in the hollow of the tubing.

3 Flux the points where the jump rings touch the tubing.

4 Cut two slightly larger solder paillons for this operation. If you're using wire solder, cut each paillon approximately 3 mm long. If you're using sheet solder, cut each paillon approximately 2 x 2 mm.

5 Using the solder pick, pick up one paillon and solder one

jump ring to the tubing. Make certain that all excess solder melts inside the tubing. Solder the second ring and tubing, and then pickle and rinse these pieces.

6 Use snips to cut the snake chain to the desired length. Flux the inside of one piece of tubing, opposite the end with the jump ring attached. Insert one end of the snake chain into the tubing as far as it will go (see photo). Do not flux the chain. (The small amount of flux brushed inside the tubing should be enough to coat the end of the chain.) Repeat this process to flux the second tube and insert the opposite end of the chain.

7 Place the chain-filled tubes on the soldering block, and space them apart. Gently heat one tube with the torch (see photo). Do not directly heat the chain with the torch. Aim all of the heat onto the tube. (The chain will get hot because it is inside the tube.) Continue to heat the tube very slowly and carefully. Keep your eye on the end of the chain that is nearest the heated tube. As soon as the chain moves on its own as if being sucked into the tubing, stop heating immediately. The excess solder that flowed into the tubing when the jump ring was attached has soldered the chain to the inside of the tube.

8 Repeat step 7 to solder the other end of the chain with its tube. Make sure the solder does not flow up the chain and freeze it at the end, because this will cause the chain to break at that point once worn. If solder flows up the chain, then the process must be repeated from the beginning.

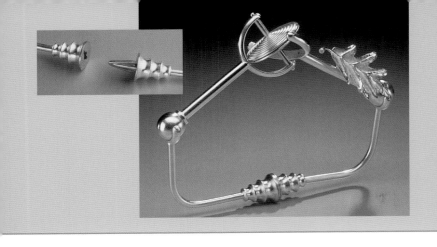

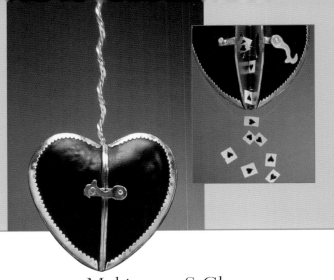

Clasps & Closures

The two essential features of good clasps and closures are that they work well and are easy to use. If a clasp does not work well, then the piece of jewelry is not secure, potentially causing loss or damage. If a clasp is not easy to use, the jewelry is less likely to be worn. Beyond security's sake, a carefully planned clasp has the ability to complement and enhance a design. For these practical and artistic reasons, you need to be very thoughtful about the type of clasp you choose for a piece.

Although there are many commercial clasps available, a handmade clasp is often the best option when making jewelry. Using a handmade clasp shows that you care about every aspect of your work and demonstrates your originality. It certainly takes more time and energy to make a handmade clasp, but the value it brings to the final product always makes the effort worthwhile.

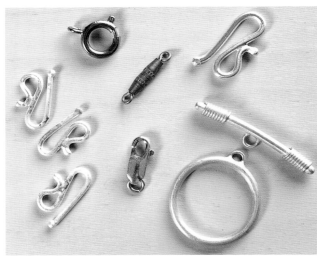

Handmade findings: S hooks, toggle clasp; commercial findings: spring ring clasp, screw clasp, lobster clasp

Making an S Clasp

The most basic handmade clasp, the S clasp with a jump ring closure, is also the simplest to make. I recommend using this design with necklaces and bracelets.

MATERIALS

Wire for jump ring and clasp, metal and gauge to complement jewelry piece

TOOLS & SUPPLIES

Bench tool kit, page 27
Soldering kit, page 27

STEP BY STEP

1 Make a jump ring with the wire of your choice and solder it closed. (You can be very creative with the type of wire you choose; try using square wire or twisting wire together. Be as elaborate as you wish with the jump ring as long as it suits the S hook and corresponds with the overall design of the piece.)

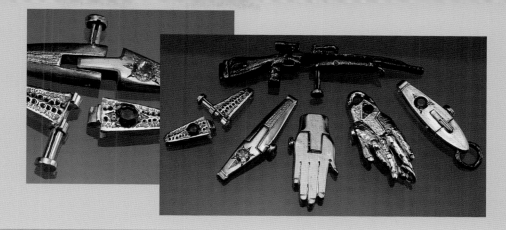

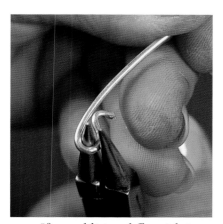

2 Cut a length of the same type of wire used for the jump ring and use round-nose pliers to bend one end into a closed U shape.

3 If an additional flourish is desired, use the round-nose pliers to bend the end of the closed U outward to make a small tail.

4 Place the round-nose pliers on the part of the wire that sticks straight out from the end of the closed U. Bend the wire in the opposite direction around the pliers to complete the S shape (see photo).

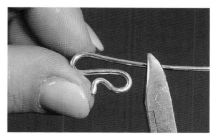

5 Use snips to cut the wire where the straight end just passes the curve of the first closed U.

6 Solder together the section of the first closed U where the wire converges. If you created a

decorative tail (step 3), solder the wire together in the curve that precedes the tail.

7 Sand the ends of the tail and the straight wire that forms the hook until they are smooth. Alternately, you can make the ends smooth by using the torch to ball up the metal at the ends of the wire (see photo).

8 Give the clasp a finish of your choice. Secure it to the jewelry piece using the French wire and crimp beads method (discussed in Simple Stringing, pages 161 and 162) or with jump rings.

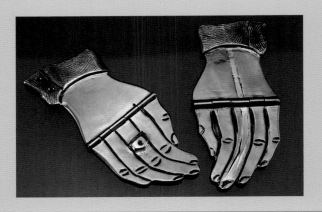

Hinges

Hinges are an outstanding way to connect links in a bracelet or a necklace, and they can be used to provide movement in a pair of earrings or on a brooch. It is very useful for jewelers to know how to make a good hinge, and there are many types of hinges you can make, such as a hidden hinge, a spring hinge, or a flush hinge. The instructions that follow are for constructing the most basic hinge.

MATERIALS

Sheet metal of your choice,
   18 gauge or thicker
Tubing, approximately 2.5 mm in
   outside diameter (OD)
Drill bit or other steel piece that
   fits perfectly inside tubing
Silver wire that telescopes perfectly
   inside tubing

TOOLS & SUPPLIES

Bench tool kit, page 27
Soldering kit, page 27
Ring clamp (optional)

STEP BY STEP

1 Use the jeweler's saw to cut two 1 x 1-inch (2.5 x 2.5 cm) squares from the sheet metal. (This small size is perfect for making a practice hinge.) File all cut edges smooth and even at a 90-degree angle.

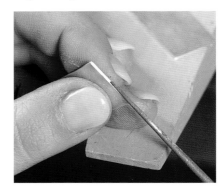

2 Using a round file, slowly file an even groove into one side of each metal square. This groove should be a half-circle deep and form a nice seat for the tubing. For easier, more secure filing, you may want to secure the sheet metal in a ring clamp.

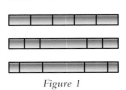

Figure 1

3 Decide whether you want to make a three- or five-knuckle hinge and determine the length of each knuckle. Figure 1 shows three design options for a five-knuckle hinge. (A hinge should always have an uneven number of knuckles.) To ensure the hinge has the proper strength, the middle knuckle should be of equal length to the outer knuckles, if not a little longer. (You can use knuckle length as a way to enhance the design of a jewelry piece. I like to make the middle knuckle a little longer than the outer knuckles, and on a five-knuckle hinge, I like the end knuckles to be the shortest ones.)

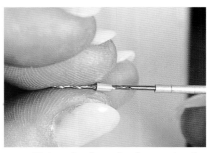

4 Using the lengths determined in step 3, cut the tubing for the knuckles with the jeweler's saw. File the cut edges perfectly flat at a 90-degree angle. (Careful sawing

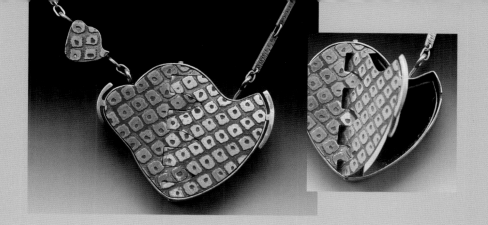

and filing is very important for making a good, tight hinge.) Insert the drill bit or other steel piece into the cut tubing, placing each knuckle close to the next one (see photo).

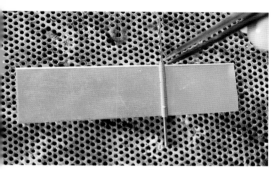

5 Position the two 1 x 1-inch (2.5 x 2.5 cm) pieces of sheet metal on the soldering block. Place the cut-tubing hinge (still on the drill bit or steel piece) between the sheet metal pieces and make sure the tubing touches both grooves filed in step 2.

6 Using a small flux brush, gently place one small drop of flux in the middle of each knuckle, alternating sides of the tubing. Do not coat the entire hinge with flux.

7 Use a pair of pliers to cut very small snippets of hard solder. (It is important that you do not use excessive amounts of solder on a hinge.) Turn on the torch, adjust the gas to form a gentle flame, and begin heating the hinge. As soon as the heated flux stops bubbling, gently use the solder pick to place one paillon of hard solder at each fluxed location in the center of each knuckle (see photo).

8 Slowly heat each knuckle in succession until the solder becomes hot enough to tack the tubing to the sheet metal. Do not let the solder flow all the way down the joint. Tack soldering the knuckles at this stage is critical to making a good hinge.

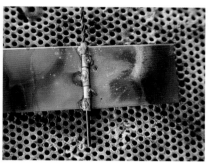

9 Once each knuckle is securely tacked to the sheet metal, turn off the torch and let the piece air cool. Do not put the piece in the pickle, because the drill bit or steel rod in the tubing will contaminate it.

10 Remove the steel rod or drill bit from the hinge, and separate its two sides. Reflux each knuckle on both sides of the hinge.

11 Turn the torch back on, keeping a gentle flame. Slowly heat each knuckle until the solder flows down the entire length of the knuckle. Once you see the solder flow, immediately take away the heat and move it to the next knuckle. Continue in this manner until each knuckle is completely soldered. This should be a fairly quick process.

12 Pickle both parts of the hinge, and then rinse and dry them. File the ends of the hinge flat so that the tubing does not extend past the width of the sheet metal (see photo).

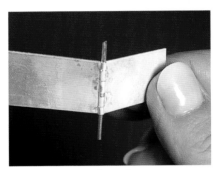

13 Insert the silver wire into the hinge, joining the two pieces together (see photo). The hinge should move freely in both directions. Use the jeweler's saw to cut the wire to a length that leaves approximately 1.5 mm extending past each end of the hinge.

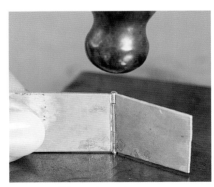

14 Rivet the wire to secure the hinge (see photo), or if you are extremely careful, solder the wire at each end of the hinge. (I only recommend soldering if you are extremely confident in your skills.) Use 400-grit sandpaper to smooth the rivet heads or the soldered ends of the hinge.

Stringing

There are many different techniques for stringing beads. To create high-quality jewelry, professional stringing methods should be followed. Fortunately, this is very easy to do, and it is well worth the extra time and effort.

Tigertail wire, assorted beading cords and threads

Types of Stringing Cord
Here are descriptions of three of the most commonly used stringing cords. I encourage you to experiment with these and with any other string or cord that strikes your fancy.

Tigertail Wire
Tigertail wire is made up of seven to 12 strands of very tiny steel wire

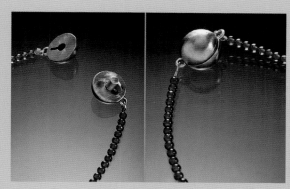

coated with a layer of plastic. It is available in several sizes. Tigertail is my favorite type of stringing wire because it is extremely durable, and it can get wet. However, if it is frequently bent, tigertail wire will eventually snap apart.

Silk Thread
Silk thread is often used for stringing nice pearls. It must be handled with care because it will fray easily, and it cannot get wet, because it will disintegrate. Silk thread also stretches, so take this into account when using it.

Polyester Thread
Polyester thread is good for stringing less expensive, natural beads. It is available in many different colors, and you can use this to your advantage in your jewelry designs. Polyester thread is not supposed to stretch, but it will eventually.

Simple Stringing

MATERIALS
Stringing cord of your choice
Crimp beads
Beads for your project
French wire*
Clasp

TOOLS & SUPPLIES
Snips
Pliers
Small nail clippers (optional)

This material is a thin, soft, and flexible metal coil. Do not confuse it with the type of ear wire that is also called a French wire.

STEP BY STEP
1   With snips, cut a length of stringing cord that is approximately 5 inches (12.7 cm) longer than the length needed for your project. (I always err on the side of caution when cutting my initial length of cord.)

2   On one end of the cord, thread a crimp bead, a project bead, another crimp bead, a section of French wire approximately ¼ inch (6 mm) long, and one section of the clasp. The length of the French wire can vary depending on the gauge of the clasp.

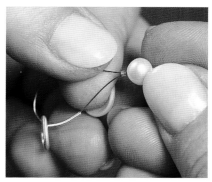

3   Make a loop in the end of the cord and rethread it through the crimp bead, the project bead, and the remaining crimp bead (see photo). Tighten the strung section so the French wire begins to bunch up a little bit. The clasp section should freely move about in the loop that is covered by the French wire.

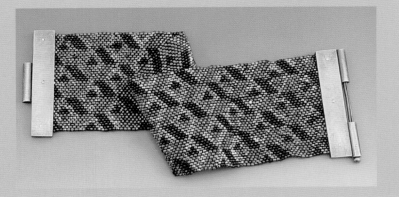

LEFT: **L. Sue Szabo**
Untitled, 2004. 0.3 x 4.2 x 17.5 cm. Sterling silver, vintage metal seed beads; hand fabricated, hinged, riveted, oxidized. Photo © Ericka Crissman, Wired Images

RIGHT: **Nicole Jacquard**
Untitled, 2001. 52 x 2.5 cm. Silver, pearls, monofilament, patina; hand fabricated, soldered, tumbled, strung. Photos © Kevin Montague

4 Use pliers to compress the crimp beads, securing them in place. Snip off the useless tail of the cord. (I find a small pair of nail clippers to be extremely useful for this purpose.)

5 String the rest of the project beads onto the cord except for one. Then thread a crimp bead, the last project bead, another crimp bead, another length of French wire, and the second section of the clasp. Make a loop in the end of the string or cord and rethread it back through the crimp bead, the project bead, and the remaining crimp bead. Tighten and secure the crimp beads. Snip off any extra string or cord.

Classic Pearl Stringing

If your design calls for the traditional type of pearl stringing and knotting, here is the technique you should follow. The most important step of pearl stringing is to finish the ends correctly and securely.

MATERIALS

Silk thread
Needle, if one is not already
    attached to the thread
Pearls
French wire
Clasp
Watch-face glue*

TOOLS & SUPPLIES

Snips
Small-nose, clean tweezers
Flexible shaft
Drill bit, 0.75 mm
Oil or beeswax

The most important thing about this particular glue is that it does not turn brittle once dry. Because it retains some play, a strand of pearls can move on the body without causing the thread to break at the point where the glue was applied. This trait is extremely important, so do not try to substitute any other type of glue, especially not two-part epoxy. The tube of watch-face glue should have a precise, needle-tip dispenser.

STEP BY STEP

1 With snips, cut a length of silk thread that is approximately 10 inches (25.4 cm) longer than the length needed for your project. Tie a simple knot approximately 5 inches (12.7 cm) from one end of the thread (see photo).

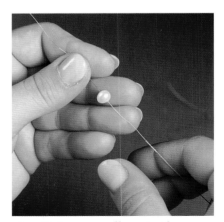

2 String a needle onto the thread if one is not already attached. Thread a pearl onto the long end of the thread.

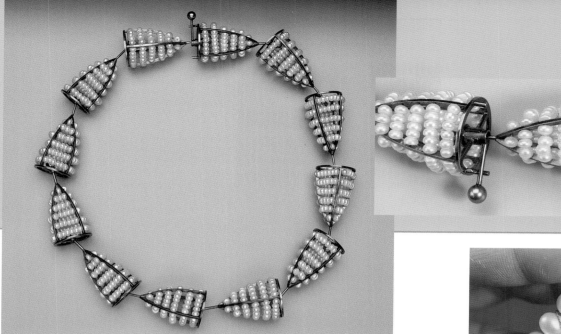

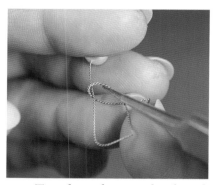

3 Tie a loose knot in the thread near the pearl. Insert the small-nose tweezers into the knot precisely as shown and hold the thread at the exact place where you want the knot to be.

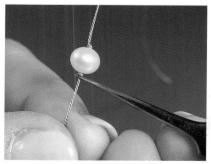

4 Pull the thread tight around the tweezers, remove the tweezers from the knot, and then use the tweezers to push the knot into place and simultaneously tighten it.

5 Continue stringing and knotting one pearl at a time until you are finished threading all but two of the pearls. (These two will go on the ends.) Remember that the clasp will add some length to the piece, so be sure to plan ahead.

6 The two reserved pearls will probably need to be drilled to enlarge the size of their holes. The holes need to be larger in order to accommodate thread being strung through the holes twice. To enlarge the hole in a pearl, use a regular, 0.75-mm drill bit coated with some oil or beeswax. Drill slowly so as not to mar the surface of the pearl. If you are stringing very expensive pearls, you may want to invest in a diamond-coated drill bit.

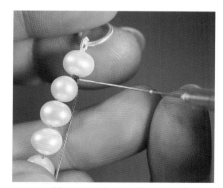

7 String one pearl on the end of the thread, and then add about 1/4 inch (6 mm) of French wire and one end of the clasp. String the thread back through the pearl, tighten the French wire, and tie a tight knot against the pearl (see photo). Leave the tail of the thread attached. Repeat this step on the other end of the piece.

8 Add a tiny drop of watch-face glue to the knots that touch the last pearls (see photo). Make sure the glue saturates the thread but does not get on the pearls. Let the glue dry for several hours. Snip off the tail of the thread on both ends of the piece.

Silver Brooch with Spiral Pin Stem

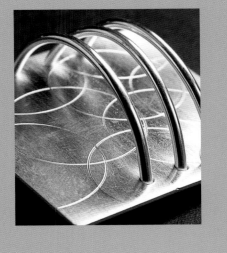

Three kinetic curved wires project above the surface of this brooch, while engraved circles repeat this motif for added appeal. The back is equally attractive with a simple, hand-fabricated pin stem.

MATERIALS

Sterling silver sheet, 18 gauge
Sterling silver round wire, 18 gauge
Sterling silver round wire, 14 gauge

TOOLS & SUPPLIES

Bench tool kit, page 27
Photocopied design template,
    page 172
Drill bit, 2 mm
Plastic circle template
Soldering kit, page 27

STEP BY STEP

1 Measure and mark a $1^1/2$ x $1^1/2$-inch (3.8 x 3.8 cm) square on the 18-gauge sterling silver sheet. Use the jeweler's saw to cut out the marked square, round the corners with a bastard file, and then sand all the corners smooth.

2 Following the photocopied design template, drill six holes at the marked locations with a 2-mm bit. Sand the silver square to a 400-grit finish.

3 Using the plastic circle template, scribe a random pattern of circles onto the front side of the silver square. (I selected a circle from the template with a $^3/4$-inch [1.9 cm] diameter.) Press hard with the scribe so the lines are deep.

4 Use the jeweler's saw to cut a $2^1/2$-inch (6.4 cm) length of the 18-gauge silver wire. Cut a second length of the wire that is 1 inch (2.5 cm) long.

5 Use round-nose pliers to make a small spiral on one end of each wire cut in step 4. Leave a tail sticking up, perpendicular to the end of each spiral.

6 Use easy solder to attach the wire spirals to the back of the silver square, approximately $1^1/4$ inches (3.2 cm) apart and 1 cm from the top of the square. The long wire should be on the right and the short wire should be on the left. (These wires will form the handmade pin stem and catch.) Pickle and rinse the piece. Remove all firescale from the silver square.

7 Use the jeweler's saw to cut three lengths of the 14-gauge sterling silver wire, each approximately $2^1/2$ inches (6.4 cm) long. One at a time, bend each wire length around a round mandrel with your fingers. The ends of the bent wires should easily fit into the holes in the silver square.

8 Insert the curved wires into the holes in the silver square, and use the torch to ball all six wire ends. The balls must be large enough to secure the wires in the holes.

9 On the back of the brooch, snip the wire tail on the left spiral approximately $^1/4$ inch (6 mm) long. Use round-nose pliers to bend the shortened tail down into a hook. This is the catch for the brooch.

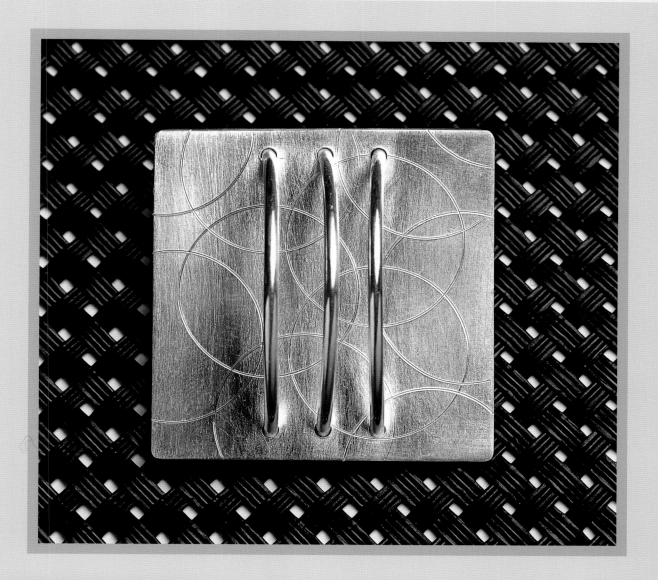

10 Bend down the tail on the right spiral, the pin stem, with round-nose pliers. Hold the location where the wire bent with round-nose pliers. Use your fingers to wrap additional wire from the tail around the nose of the pliers in an upward motion to make a circle with the wire that is parallel to the surface of the metal square. Shape the tail to hook into the catch formed in step 9.

11 Snip off extra wire from the pin stem and file the end of the wire to a point that will easily slide through fabric. Sand the pointed wire end to a 400-grit finish.

12 Give the brooch a final finish, taking care not to harm the scribed circles. (I used heavy-grit steel wool to create a partially shiny finish.)

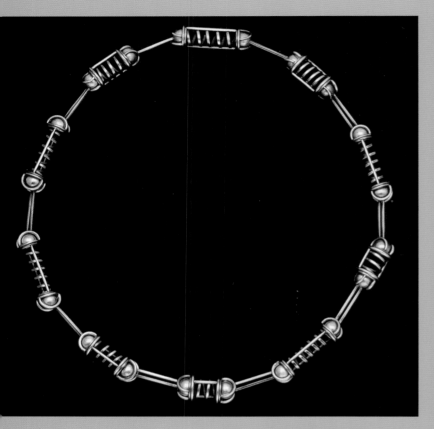

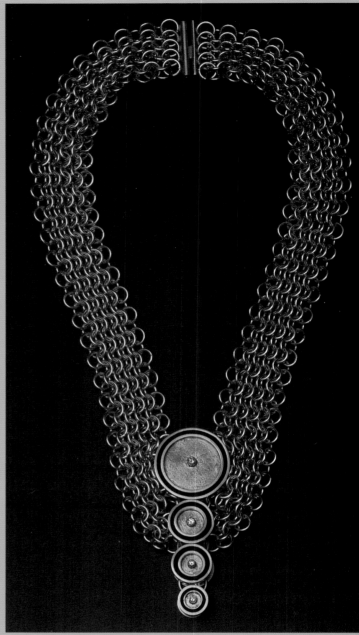

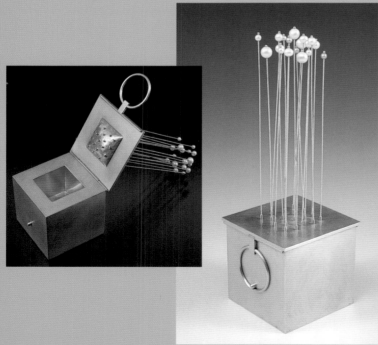

TOP LEFT: **Christina Lemon**
No Missing Links?, 1994. 63.5 cm long.
Sterling silver, patina; fabricated. Photo © artist

TOP RIGHT: **Christine Dhein**
White Nile Neckpiece #2, 2000. 26.5 x 10 x 0.6 cm. 24-karat gold,
14-karat gold, sterling silver, rubber, diamonds; hand fabricated, riveted,
kum boo, tube set. Photo © Don Felton

BOTTOM LEFT: RIGHT: **Junghyun Woo**
Sharing I, 2004. 17 x 5 x 5 cm. 24-karat gold, 18-karat gold, sterling
silver, pearls, guitar string; kum boo, die formed, hand fabricated,
oxidized. Photos © Helen Shirk

TOP LEFT: Carol Fugmann
Untitled, 1999. 50.8 cm long. Sterling silver, 14-karat gold; hand fabricated. Photo © Terry Anthony

TOP RIGHT: Felicity Peters
My Life in Black & White, Each element, 2002. 2.5 x 2.5 x 0.5 cm. Sterling silver, paper; laminated. Photo © Victor France

CENTER RIGHT: Ericia Bartels-Dawkins
Untitled, 2005. 8 x 5 x 3 cm. Sterling silver, rubies; hollow formed, riveted, fabricated. Photo © Tom Madden

BOTTOM RIGHT: Patricia Madeja
Slinky Necklace, 1997. 43 x 2 x 2 cm. Sterling silver links, 14-karat white gold; cast, assembled, hand finished. Photo © Ralph Gabriner

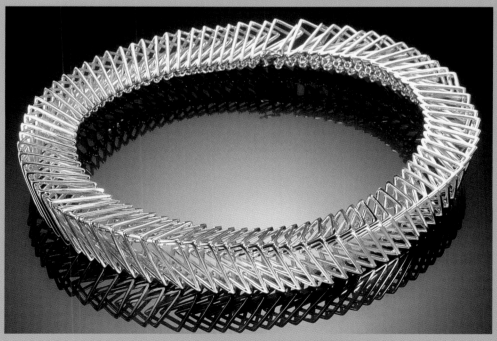

Metal Clay

Making jewelry with metal clay has many creative and convenient qualities that traditional metal fabrication does not. Metal clay is incredibly malleable, allowing it to be quickly textured with limitless surface treatments, and using metal clay allows you to make large jewelry pieces without the weight of conventionally cast objects. Composed of water, an organic binder, and particles of precious metal (silver or gold), metal clay can be sculpted like regular clay and holds infinite design possibilities.

MATERIALS
Slow-fire metal clay

TOOLS & SUPPLIES
Variety of knives, such as plastic knives and craft knives
Plastic rolling pin
Any sort of material that has texture
Bench tool kit, page 27
Kiln with pyrometer
Clean soldering pad or terra-cotta saucer
Vermiculite or alumina hydrate
Soldering kit, page 27

STEP BY STEP

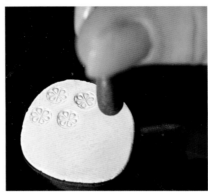

1 Use your fingers or tools, such as knives, a rolling pin, textured material, or items from your bench tool kit, to form the metal clay into the shape you desire. See Bench Tips for ideas and techniques. Set the piece aside and allow it to dry completely overnight. (Smaller objects may have a shorter drying time. To test a piece for dryness, rest it on your hand. If the piece is at all cool or clammy, it is probably not dry.)

2 Consult the metal clay manufacturer's instructions for the appropriate firing temperatures, and heat the kiln (approximately 1650°F [898.9°C] for silver metal clay and 1830°F [998.9°C] for gold metal clay). Place the dry, sculpted metal clay piece on some type of kiln support. Flat objects can be placed on a clean soldering pad or a simple terra-cotta saucer. Three-dimensional objects should rest in vermiculite (found at gardening stores) as shown in photo A

RIGHT: **Celie Fago**
Pierced Pod Pendant, 2004. 70 x
1.5 x 0.8 cm . Fine silver metal clay,
18-karat royal gold, 24-karat gold
foil, sterling silver, patina; formed,
constructed, fired, kum boo.
Photo © Robert Diamante

FAR RIGHT: **Shahasp Valentine**
Grande Fleur-de-Lis Necklace #6,
2001. 2.8 x 3.5 x 0.6 cm. Fine
silver metal clay, rubies; hand
formed, fired. Photo © Hap Sakwa

or alumina hydrate (available from clay suppliers), because these granular supports help the pieces with stand the heat of firing. Place the piece in the kiln (photo B) and fire it at an even temperature for a full 2 hours or as directed by the metal clay manufacturer.

3 Remove the fully fired metal clay piece from the kiln, and let it cool. The piece will have a whitish appearance. Sanding and finishing will easily remove this white oxide (see photo).

4 Solder any necessary jewelry findings onto the fired piece. If needed, pickle and rinse after soldering, and then finish the piece as desired.

BENCH TIPS

To repair any cracks or splits, simply mix water with metal clay to form a slip. (A slip is simply a watered-down version of the thicker, tougher metal clay.) Paint the slip into any crack or split in the dry clay, allow the slip to dry completely, and then fire the piece.

Metal clay shrinks. After firing, you can expect a piece to have shrunk about 28 percent from its original size.

While the metal clay is wet, you can use a straw to make a hole in the surface. (Save any extra material, because you can rewet it and use it later.) You can also drill the metal clay after it has been fired to make holes.

Use two spacers to make an even metal-clay sheet. Spacers can be any type of sheet metal, playing cards, or mat board. Arrange the spacers so the distance between their edges is the width of the clay sheet you want to make. Place a ball of clay between the spacers, and roll it with a slightly oiled plastic rolling pin (olive oil works well) until you have an even sheet.

To make a perfect "snake," roll out a length of metal clay in your hands, and place it between two slightly oiled pieces of glass. Roll the top piece of glass back and forth on the snake to create an equal diameter for the entire length of the clay.

To add texture to the metal clay, an infinite variety of objects can be used. Simply press the source of the texture into the clay until the imprint is deep enough. Make sure the clay is sufficiently moist when texturing, but not overly moist.

To join metal clay pieces together, use a paintbrush and some slip. Gently run the slip-filled brush along the joints until they are sealed.

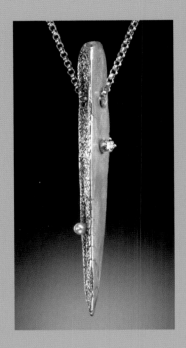

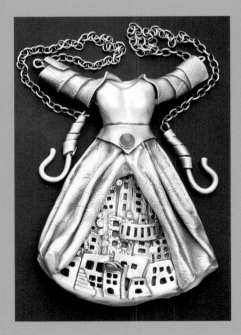

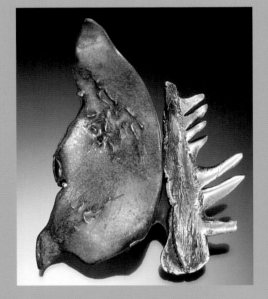

TOP LEFT: **Shahasp Valentine**
Knife Edge Necklace #17, 2003. 5.4 x 0.6 x 0.6 cm. Fine silver, 24-karat gold metal clay, diamond, pearl; hand formed, prong set. Photo © Hap Sakwa

TOP RIGHT: **Barbara Becker Simon**
The Maltese Fish, 2000. 55 x 40 x 20 cm. Fine silver metal clay bead and clasp, synthetic sapphires, freshwater pearls, seed beads, sterling silver. Photo © Larry Sanders

BOTTOM LEFT: **Hadar Jacobson**
City Dress, 2004. 12 x 7 x 2 cm. Fine silver metal clay, labradorite, synthetic yellow sapphire, cubic zirconia; hand fabricated, fired, oxidized, finished. Photo © artist

BOTTOM CENTER: **Leni Fuhrman**
Jaw Carapace, 2005. 7 x 5 x 1 cm. Silver metal clay, enamel, copper, sterling silver, patina; hand fabricated, torch fired, oxidized. Photo © Ralph Gabriner

BOTTOM RIGHT: **Pamela Morris Thomford**
Sneaky Pete, 2001. 8 x 3 x 2.5 cm. Sterling silver, fine silver, fine silver metal clay; hand fabricated, cast, roller printed. Photo © Keith Meiser

TOP LEFT: Barbara Becker Simon
Pinctada Maximus, 2004. 22 x 20 x 9 cm.
Fine silver metal clay, fine gold metal clay,
pearls, glass beads; constructed, fired. Photo ©
Larry Sanders

TOP RIGHT: Celie Fago
Locket Pendant, 2004. 3.8 cm in diameter.
Fine silver metal clay, 18-karat royal gold, 24-
karat gold foil, 23-karat gold leaf, sterling silver,
polymer clay, patina; photo transfer, formed,
constructed, fired, kum boo, collage. Photos ©
Robert Diamante

CENTER RIGHT: Celie Fago
Hollow Form Box Bracelet, 2004. Each element, 2 x 2.2 x 0.7 cm. Fine silver metal clay,
18-karat royal gold, 24-karat gold foil, patina;
formed, constructed, fired, kum boo, hinged.
Photo © Robert Diamante

BOTTOM RIGHT: Shahasp Valentine
Opera Necklace #1, 1999. Length adjustable,
35.6 to 43.2 cm. Fine silver, precious metal
clay, sapphire, zircon, iolite, freshwater pearls;
hand formed, fired. Photo © Hap Sakwa

Templates

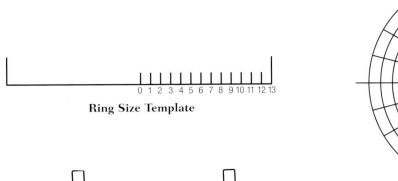

Ring Size Template

Circle Divider Template

Reversible Pendant, page 60

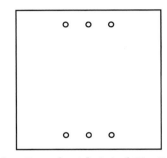

Silver Brooch with Spiral Pin Stem
page 164

Filigree Pendant
page 112

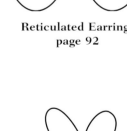

Reticulated Earrings
page 92

Template A

Template B

Template C

Marriage of Metal Bracelet, page 128

Contributing Artists

Acknowledgments

Thanks to my jeweler friends for sharing their knowledge. I am especially indebted to Steve Midgett, Joan Bazzel, Lori Talcott, and Douglas Harling. Thanks to Geoff Giles for his patience and for sharing the studio so generously.

Thanks to the wonderful people at Lark Books—to my dream editor, Marthe Le Van; to Kathy Holmes for her tasteful and beautiful art direction; to Keith Wright for his fabulous photography and humor; to Barbara Zaretsky for her gorgeous cover; to Nathalie Mornu for her work behind the scenes; and to Terry Taylor for his loyal support.

Thanks to Billy Valentine, Kate Calto, Meredith Greene, and Jody Watkins for their continuous support and encouragement.

About the Author

Joanna Gollberg is a studio artist in Asheville, North Carolina. She enjoys making many types of metal work, especially jewelry, which she exhibits at galleries and craft fairs throughout the United States. Joanna is a graduate of the Fashion Institute of Technology with a degree in jewelry design, and has taught workshops at the Penland School of Crafts and the John C Campbell Folk School. She is the author of two other Lark books, *Making Metal Jewelry* and *Creative Metal Crafts*.

Index